MAKING JESUS KNOWN

SCRIPTURE UNION STORIES
FROM AROUND THE WORLD

MICHAEL HEWS

SCRIPTURE UNION
130 CITY ROAD, LONDON EC1V 2NJ

© Michael Hews 1995

First published 1995

ISBN 0 86201 891 9

All rights reserved. No part of this publication may be reproduced, stored in a retrieval system, or transmitted, in any form or by any means, electronic, photocopying, recording, or otherwise, without the prior permission of Scripture Union.

The right of Michael Hews to be identified as author of this work has been asserted by him in accordance with the Copyright, Designs and Patents Act 1988.

Cover photo: Mike Perks
Cover design: Tony Cantale Graphics

British Library Cataloguing-in-Publication Data
A catalogue record for this book is available from the British Library.

Phototypeset by Intype, London.
Printed and bound in Great Britain by Cox & Wyman Ltd, Reading.

CONTENTS

Introduction	5
ON A ROCK IN THE TROPICS Clayton Fergie *Australia*	9
A REASON FOR LIVING Paulina Barrera *Chile*	20
'I HEARD THE GENTLE WHISPER OF GOD' Lydia Trnkova *Czech Republic*	27
'I'M A HUMAN BEING AS WELL' Andy Saunders *England*	36
'WE'VE NEVER MISSED OUT ON ANYTHING' Daniel Agopian *France*	46
THE GIFT OF LAUGHTER Renate Franz *Germany*	55
WHERE SLAVERY'S LEGACY LINGERS Gene Denham *Jamaica*	63
'I'VE FOUND JESUS' Comfort Essien *Nigeria*	73
'I TEND TO GRAVITATE TO THOSE WHO ARE FAILURES' Joe Campbell *Northern Ireland*	80

'I WAS STAGGERED THAT GOD HAD USED ME' 93
Janice Aiton *Scotland*

NO BASKING IN PAST GLORIES 101
Mona Chia *Singapore*

BROWN WORLD, WHITE WORLD, BLACK WORLD 109
Daryl Henning, Mike Perks, Mgi Mabuza
South Africa

INTRODUCTION

I confess to being an enthusiast, and this book springs from three of my enthusiams.

This is a people book, and I'm enthusiastic about the people whose stories it tells. Some I have interviewed face to face, others through an exchange of audio tapes across the world. But in every conversation, live or on tape, that has gone into the making of this book, I have sensed the warmth of the friendship of brothers and sisters in Christ.

These are stories that deserve to be told – and at greater length than is possible in a magazine article. They are the stories of people who would never claim to be Christian megastars, but who have seen God at work in their lives and in the ministries in which they are engaged. These are courageous people, who are representative of many more Scripture Union staff members whom I have been privileged to meet.

SU is a family

For I confess that after nearly forty years on the staff, I am still unashamedly enthusiastic about the SU movement – and not least because it is a genuinely international movement, and there aren't too many of those around!

It wasn't always exactly like that. The SU movement began in England in 1867 in the heyday of the British Empire, and in its early years it was sometimes guilty of exporting rather more than the gospel.

The pioneers of the movement certainly had a global vision. For example, between 1877 and 1893, they distributed thirteen million leaflets for children in fifty different languages. But whilst they translated the words, they didn't change the very English illustrations.

So the leaflet in the language of Tahiti contained a marvellous line-drawing of some primly Victorian, voluminously-clad English boys and girls sheltering under an umbrella. Thus were the children in the South Pacific taught not only the gospel but also the customs of the English in the rainy season.

But all that was long ago. Today the SU movement in Pakistan is run by Pakistanis and the SU movement in Mexico by Mexicans. SU's International Secretary is a Nigerian and the Chairman of the International Council is from German-speaking Switzerland.

SU is a family of national SU movements in more than a hundred countries. It's a family that accepts that Christians in different cultures will express their faith and commitment in different ways. It's a family that is firmly against cultural imperialism, firmly committed to racial equality and to the unity of Christian believers of all races.

A celebration of international unity . . .

This book is a kind of celebration of that international unity. It's not only a unity in doctrine. There's an SU flavour that pervades the movement worldwide. To quote one of SU's working principles, the movement aims 'to express God's good news to children, young people and families, not only in words, but also by building caring relationships with them'.

. . . and cultural diversity

It's fascinating also to see how basic concepts like that of the camp and that of the voluntary school Christian group have been adopted (with all kinds of variations) in so many countries and cultures.

'Camp' in the language of SU worldwide means far more than a collection of tents or cabins used by holiday-makers. A Scripture Union camp is a place where for a weekend or a week or more, leaders and young people share their lives, for twenty-four hours a day, in such a way that the good news of Jesus can be powerfully demonstrated as well as proclaimed. Across the world, there are an enormous variety of camp venues, camp programmes, camp cuisines – but at the heart of each there is a Christian community. (I'm aware, of course, that some SU movements use the term 'holiday' rather than 'camp'.)

Voluntary school Christian groups are almost as varied.

Some sing a lot, some don't sing at all. Some are called Scripture Union groups, some are called ISCF (Inter-School Christian Fellowship) groups, some have other names. All have to confront the need to relate biblical truth to the burning issues of the day with which young people in their country and culture are having to grapple.

But all are groups where Christians can encourage one another and can share their faith. And they function in a world where few go inside a church but nearly everyone goes to school, and where being a Christian at school can be hard going.

Invited to speak for themselves

This is truly an international book. It features fourteen SU staff members, all of whom God has called to serve in their own countries. They have been invited to speak for themselves. If we are to have a clearer vision of a world in need, we have to listen to Christian voices from beyond our own country and our own culture.

The gospel, a multi-faceted diamond

My wife and I once took some South African friends to see the Crown Jewels in the Tower of London. As we walked slowly round the showcases, we were able to view these priceless treasures from different angles. There in front of us were large, chunky multi-faceted diamonds, and as we moved round, different facets of those diamonds sparkled according to our position. It has occurred to me since that, although there is only one gospel, that gospel is a bit like a diamond: different facets of it sparkle for different people according to their situation.

This book tells of many faith journeys. And for many of those whose journeys it describes, there was one facet that sparkled when they first saw the diamond. Maybe it was the facet of forgiveness or the facet of acceptance or the facet of joining the biggest family in the world. And then, when they responded to the gospel by committing their lives to Christ as Saviour and Lord, they began to see that there were more facets of the gospel diamond than they ever had realised.

But diamonds are not for ever. And to liken the gospel to a cold, lifeless jewel is hopelessly inadequate. For the gospel is the good news of Jesus.

Michael Hews

ON A ROCK IN THE TROPICS

Clayton Fergie

AUSTRALIA

Clayton Fergie was probably the first busker to be invited to join the Scripture Union staff.

The youngest of five in a Christian family, he arrived six years after No 4. 'My mum cried when she found she was pregnant with me. I assume they were tears of joy!'

He may not have been planned, but he was certainly loved. Inevitably, as he was the youngest, 'my brothers and sisters and particularly Gill, my eldest sister, had quite a lot to do with my rearing.'

He was born in Adelaide but his parents moved back to Canberra when he was very young. One of his earliest childhood memories is of playing cricket under the trees in the family backyard. 'We had a fig tree and a mulberry and an apricot.'

He has happy memories of childhood holidays, too. 'My father was a fanatical camper. We used to go off as a family in a combi van with a canoe on our roof-rack and often with a sailing boat in a trailer behind. He'd equipped the van with a kind of kitchenette – with a gas stove and an icebox. This was back in the early 60s.'

Clayton also had the enrichment of a multi-cultural childhood. When he was nine or ten, his father, who was a statistician, was seconded to a lecturing assignment for the United Nations in Japan.

In Hong Kong, tears of helplessness

'That was a major culture shock. We flew to Hong Kong en route for Tokyo, and it was in Hong Kong that I had my first encounter with poverty. We went by taxi to have a meal at a floating restaurant, and outside the restaurant were some boys selling trinkets. I understood that this was their bread and butter, this was how they made a living, but my parents were cautious about letting me buy anything because they were afraid I would be ripped off.

'When we came out of the restaurant after our meal, these kids were still there. I desperately wanted to buy some of their trinkets, but I wasn't allowed to. I remember, as we drove away, watching them from the back of our taxi in tears. They were tears of helplessness.

'In Japan I went to an American Catholic school, and that was quite an experience for a truly Protestant Aussie kid. And our parents took us round the country. We often stayed in youth hostels, and we saw lots of Japanese temples. We made a great many friends.

'When we came home from Japan, we were only in Australia for six months before we set off for Papua New Guinea. We were there for four years. It felt like a lifetime, because it was an extremely important part of my life, and I have so many fond memories of PNG. It was there that I came to personal faith in Christ and it was there that I met the girl who was to become my wife.'

In Papua New Guinea, a coffee shop with fishing nets

'Our family went to Boroko Baptist Church in PNG's capital, Port Moresby. The church had a coffee shop for young people during the school holidays. It had fishing nets hanging from the ceilings and candles on the tables, and it served raisin and cinnamon toast, with Milo, tea and coffee. I heard people talking about their faith as a personal thing, and I came to the point where I wanted to commit my life to Christ. I remember asking a guy who was one of the leaders to pray with me.'

'At thirteen, I had my eye on my future wife'

'In PNG we had a tremendous ISCF (Inter-School Christian Fellowship) group at high school. Between fifty and eighty kids met regularly.

'When I was in my first year, someone proposed that I should be on the committee. So I suggested that a girl called Lisa England should be on the committee too. At the age of thirteen, I already had my eye on my future wife.'

Clayton remembers going to an Easter Scripture Union camp in PNG. 'I was almost the only white kid there. I remember an early morning service in a grassy area surrounded by jungle. There was dew on the ground, though of course it was quite warm because we were in the tropics. I remember sitting there among so many black Christians and having this incredible sense of being part of God's culturally diverse family. For a thirteen year old to have those experiences was just fantastic.

'In those days in PNG the Spirit of God was really moving. It was close to revival.

'When I came back to Australia as a fourteen or fifteen year old, it was like walking into a brick wall. The youth groups seemed very stagnant. But my faith remained strong. I was one of the very few males in our ISCF group in high school. I could cope with that because my heart was really back in PNG with Lisa. At the age of fourteen or fifteen, we were deeply in love.'

Clayton remembers that in his teenage years he questioned Western values and questioned the church. But he held firm to his core beliefs.

'Are you willing to give up your security?'

Clayton confesses, 'I've always been a fairly loud-mouthed, self-confident, big, dominant Aussie male. So I've always tended to exercise leadership roles, though I think that's become refined over the years.

'Late one night when I was at university, I was listening to a music tape of a Christian concert, and there was a speaker who was talking about Jesus walking on the water.

He made the point that out of all the guys in that boat Peter was the only one who was willing to give up his security. And he went on to say "What's your security? How willing are you to give that up and to get out maybe into a storm to follow Jesus?"

'I knew that was God challenging me. I was training to be a teacher. That was my security and God was saying "Are you willing to give up that and to do things the way I want you to do them?"

'So I decided that I would withdraw from the teaching course and wait for God. But the question was, how would we survive? At that time Lisa and I had recently been married, and her parents had given us a book of Bible readings as a wedding present. That night we turned to the reading for the day and we read, "If I care for the birds of the air, how much more will I care for you."'

One day, over the washing up...

'Well, it was crazy, but the next day I withdrew from the teaching course. When we told our pastor what I had done, he was very affirming.

'I wouldn't necessarily recommend that anyone else should do what we did – my wife and I love adventure!

'I should explain that I worked part-time at a child care centre. I'd also been involved in a band. One day over the washing-up, the idea came to me that I should go out on the street and become a busker, singing Christian songs.

'I firmly believe that was God's purpose for me.'

Living 'on baked beans and stuff like that'

'It's interesting that ten years later, when I was on the SU staff here in the Northern Territory, we had a difficult time financially. For several months full salaries couldn't be paid. We often lived on baked beans and stuff like that. It was hard, and one day we turned to the book of Bible readings that we'd been given when we were married. It was the same reading, "If I care for the birds of the air...", all over again. It turned out to be ten years to the day since we'd first read those words on the night we decided I should give up my teaching course.

'I busked for a year. I learnt a lot about singing! Then to my surprise a friend told me "I've given your name to Scripture Union for the position of schools worker."

'I didn't know about the position, but SU had been part of my life. I'd had contact with a beach mission as a kid. The then General Secretary of SU in PNG had had a considerable impact on me when I was there – and there'd been the link through the ISCF groups.

'So I applied to the SU Council in ACT (Australian Capital Territory) and eventually I was employed part-time. I was very green and a bit unlikely.'

Later, his appointment became full time, and when his boss in SU in ACT was ill for several months, he was asked to take over as Acting Director.

When a vacancy arose for a Director for SU in the Northern Territory, it was suggested that Clayton should apply. 'They were looking for someone who would adapt to the lifestyle of the tropics and who had experience of working with people of other cultures. They were also looking for a family person, and I seemed to fit the bill.

A place of adventure, complete with crocodiles

'Lisa and I love the Northern Territory. It's similar in many ways to PNG, so it brings back childhood memories. It's a place of adventure.'

Last year, Clayton's family and some friends from Canberra went camping one night at a hot spring 'down the track'. When they had put the kids to bed, the grown-ups went off for a swim, only to find themselves standing amongst some crocodiles. 'We ran in all directions.... Later we went back with a video camera and counted six of them.' A place of adventure indeed.

'The Northern Territory is also remote. It's a huge area – one-fifth of the Australian continent with a population of only 165,000. I enjoy the pioneering aspect. We're a pioneering family. We love the countryside – it's very hot, hostile, rocky, dry.

'Darwin, the capital, has a population of only 75,000. And it takes five days to drive from Darwin to Canberra, our home city. In the Northern Territory a long day's drive is 1100 kilometres, and we've done that seven times with our five kids. Recently I travelled a total of 700 kilometres for a three-hour meeting. And that wasn't the first time.'

'We're sick to death of coconuts'

'We live in the Darwin suburb of Nightcliff in a four-bedroom, one-storey house which is provided by Scripture Union. It's a great family house, with a long hallway which is a good racing track for our kids' tricycles.

'We have three or four coconut trees in our backyard. We're sick to death of coconuts.'

'I love it when young people come to Christ'

Clayton obviously enjoys the work that God has called him to do. He enjoys resourcing other Christian people, and he enjoys being in front-line ministry himself. 'I love it when young people come to Christ. I love seeing young people changed. I love helping kids understand that my Saviour is real.

'I love Question Time in Christian Option programmes.'

Along with SU movements in some other Australian states, SU in the Northern Territory is in action in the high schools, not only through voluntary ISCF groups, but also in classroom teaching.

As Clayton explains, 'Our Christian Option programmes are a combination of religious and social education. We develop lessons which dovetail with the teaching the students are getting and which communicate the gospel.'

He gives us an example: 'If they're studying post-war Australian history, we would look at changes in beliefs and values since the Second World War. We would look at three generations: those who were involved in the war; the "baby-boomers", who were influenced, for example, by Vietnam and the Pill; and the current generation, who are particularly into environmental issues. We would talk about Christian value systems. We would look at the constants and get into the gospel.'

'We struggle with the idea of long-term commitment'

'In our Christian Option programmes as well as in our camps, we work hard to get kids to have hands-on experience with the Bible. We hand out a lot of free gospels.'

Generally, however, Clayton finds it difficult to promote Bible reading. 'Ours is not only a post-literate society but also a society that struggles with the idea of long-term commitment. The whole concept of our growing as Christians bit by bit, day by day – which is at the heart of the Scripture Union method of regular Bible reading – is foreign to my generation and to my children's generation.

'I have the gut feeling that the tide will turn. I come across more and more people who are seeing the folly of not making Bible reading a priority. They've seen what can happen when Christians of long standing are still biblically illiterate.'

'Being his at school'

Group Bible studies are the staple diet of some of the voluntary ISCF groups in Australian high schools. But there's quite a diversity amongst the groups. There's no standard model. 'It's like a football field. There are boundaries. But a variety of games can be played on the field.

'School is a microcosm of society, and we promote ISCF with the basic idea that it's to help kids – and teachers and support staff too – to be God's people, in their schools. We use the term "Being his at school".

'Sometimes that means helping them to survive. It's not easy for young Christians in school. For others who are further on in their faith journey, it means helping them to put their beliefs into practice, and to evangelise their friends in an appropriate way. I believe that evangelism is – or should be – a natural outcome of a close relationship with God. So it's our priority to help kids develop that relationship.

'I can think of two ISCF groups here in Darwin. One is a small group. Evangelism isn't on their agenda, but survival and companionship are. They have Bible studies, games and the occasional speaker, and they need the encouragement of being a Christian presence together in the school.

'In another school, the ISCF group is much larger. A number of Christian teachers and local church youth leaders are involved in it. They have several meetings a week to respond to different needs. One is designed for Christians. But they also run a coffee shop where they serve free iced coffee and chocolate. It's a drop-in place. There is some spiritual input, but it's really a bridge-building ministry.'

'Helping local churches achieve mission'

Clayton's vision is that SU's role in all this 'is to help churches to achieve mission effectively. Not to do things for the churches, or in spite of them, but with them – by providing materials, training, encouragement, by working in partnership – so that they can do a better job.'

Clayton is deeply committed to the principle that SU is a volunteer movement, with a comparatively small number of staff motivating and training a much larger number of volunteers.

In fulfilment of Clayton's vision for SU in the Northern Territory, the movement's camping strategy is mainly to resource local churches. It works this way. A small group of SU volunteers organises the camp. They do all the logistics and market the camp to church youth leaders. Groups of church kids come with their non-Christian mates. They bring their own food and tents, though Clayton adds reassuringly, 'We have spare tent pegs and spares of most things – and if a group needs help in cooking a meal, we'll give it.'

'Cathedral experience' without the hassle

It's a strategy that's particularly effective because there are a number of churches with small youth groups. This way they can go camping with the minimum of hassle. They can all have what Clayton calls the 'cathedral experience', and then the youth leaders go back with their kids and are there to nurture and encourage them. This is one way SU in the Northern Territory helps local churches to engage in mission.

What, in Clayton's view, is the 'magic' of camps? 'They provide a compact temporary community. You have leaders who are highly committed, quality people who are very focused. Kids are put through a community process which ranges from cleaning your teeth with your leaders to having outrageous fun with them. And you have some terrific, deep and meaningful discussions about all sorts of topics that the leaders have already thought through. It's a quality event.

'In SU we're not on about manipulating people. We're on about helping kids to think through life options. And that's exactly what happens. Kids are presented with the gospel, not just verbally but in a lifestyle. They see leaders at their best and worst. They see the reactions of Christians when you drop a brick on their foot.

'This deep sense of community is as much the liability of camps as it is their genius. We have to help kids to get back into real life when the camp is over.

'Camps have been a key element in the conversion of many, many kids that I have known.'

'Aussies don't normally sing like that unless they're drunk'

Clayton recalls a Leadership Training Camp that was an outstanding experience. Young people with leadership potential took part in this event, studying Paul's letter to the Philippians, and having skills training. They were also involved in groups in initiative tests. And they experienced community living.

'Late one evening one of the young men shared very openly about the times when he'd been put down because he was short. He was in tears, and others in the group got round him and prayed for him.

'Now it's in the nature of Aussie males to be macho, and it's hard to get them to share openly, let alone to cry. This incident broke through all that. And later that night the twelve guys in the male dormitory started to sing worship songs – and in three-part harmony! I've never seen anything like it in this country before. Aussies don't normally sing like that unless they're really drunk!'

'Aussie kids faced with so many cultures and beliefs'

But Clayton reminds us that Australia is now a multi-cultural society. For example, ten percent of the population of Darwin is Greek. In the Northern Territory, there are also many Asians as well as white Anglo-Saxons and there are the aboriginal communities.

'Behind me on the beach as I talk to you, there are two men walking with their dogs. They're chatting to each other. One is obviously of Indian descent. The other is a white Anglo-Saxon. This symbolises Australia as it is today.

'Aussie kids are faced with so many cultures, so many beliefs and value systems, and they are all presented in schools as of equal worth. They are obviously also influenced by contemporary music, by the subtleties of materialism and by the advocacy of safe sex.' And Clayton's experience of the Christian Option programmes leads him to believe that the question that Aussie young people are really asking is 'What is truth? What are we to believe? How can I make sense of all this?'

Clayton has found that 'If you can break the ice, there is incredible interest in the Christian gospel.'

'Ours is a hurting country'

But he also points out that Australians have a history of being sceptical. 'That goes back to our historical roots. We have a history of rejection. Many of our ancestors were dumped here as convicts, and their sceptical attitude to authority is still around. Others came here more recently, looking to make a new beginning. Then we have our indigenous aboriginal minority, and there are aboriginals around today whose grandparents can tell them horrific stories of the cruelty they suffered at the hands of the white men.

'Ours is a hurting country.' Clayton says what is left unsaid in the Australian soaps exported to TV screens around the world.

'Our grandparents fought for the British Empire, an empire thousands of miles away. The two world wars helped to focus our identity as Australians. But since then we have become a multi-cultural nation, and today in schools I meet kids whose grandparents came from Vietnam or Italy.

'And we are still struggling to have a national identity. We struggle to be proud of who we are. We live in the shadow and guilt of the terrible way we treated aboriginal people. We struggle now to know how to deal with that and how to deal with our regional neighbours.

'We've just come through thirty years of "boom" – and now we're in the biggest recession in fifty years. And there aren't the secure family networks there used to be. One Australian marriage in four breaks down.

'Young people are facing a confused situation. No longer are they assured of getting jobs, no longer are they assured of having caring families...

'As I talk about this, I find myself with tears in my eyes. We really are a hurting group of people.'

'Jesus loves you, no matter what'

So what above all else, I asked Clayton, is the good news for the young people of Australia, where so many beliefs and value systems are on offer?

His answer from that tropical beach: 'The good news is that our Christian values are based on the person of Jesus Christ, about whom we have an historical account in the gospels.

'As I often say to children and teenagers in schools, "Jesus loves you, no matter what, and he wants you to love him." We can find truth, meaning, purpose and direction in Jesus Christ.'

A REASON FOR LIVING

Paulina Barrera

CHILE

Paulina Barrera is a pastor's daughter. She is the youngest of a family of six. 'It was almost as if I was the child of my older brothers and sisters. I grew up being aware that I was very much loved – but at the same time I wasn't too sheltered. In my home, I was always being told, "You're really special. You matter." '

Paulina's father, who died seven years ago, had a profound influence on her life. 'From an early age I was made to understand that I had a great responsibility to the Lord. I grew up with that always in mind.'

Rebel against hypocrisy

Did she ever rebel as a teenager? 'Against God, no. But I rebelled against hypocrisy, especially amongst church people. Against people in leadership positions whose faith was not worked out in their daily lives.'

Paulina's intense dislike of hypocrisy remains to this day. But at school she faced a very different kind of problem. She went to a private school where almost all the pupils were Roman Catholics. 'The whole of my class knew I was an evangelical and they rejected me. It was quite tough. (In Chile at that time, evangelicals were verbally persecuted. It's different now; evangelicals are no longer considered heretics by the Roman Catholic Church, they're separated brethren.)

Being a Christian in a world that rejects you

'I couldn't see any support for children who were up against this kind of pressure. That's what made me go into teaching. I wanted to help young people with the problems of being a Christian in a world that rejects you. And even today, few young people at school will admit they are evangelicals for fear of rejection.'

Paulina attended the first SU training workshop ever held in Chile. She became a volunteer supporter of school SU groups, and a while later was invited to join the staff of SU Chile (which has camping, training, Bible reading and literature ministries besides schools work) as General Secretary – for 'one year'. That was six years ago!

'We have no history of schools work in Chile' – it's been a pioneering task and a struggle. And sadly, many evangelical Christian young people avoid the groups because they've been taught to avoid anything that isn't organised by their particular church.

The groups are led by SU staff or volunteers, and SU has endeavoured to give greater responsibility for the groups to volunteers from local churches. But the churches have been slow to catch the vision for systematic ministry in schools, and there's often too limited a concept of what a responsible volunteer ought to be and to do.

'To know they are valued by God'

But by 1992 there were SU groups with regular weekly meetings in ten schools in Santiago and in three others to the North. The aim of the groups is get young people 'to hear and to appropriate the truth that God loves them and wants to have a relationship with them, and to know that they are valued by God and that there is a reason for which they are alive.'

Many Chilean young people, says Paulina, have a sense of aimlessness. She believes this is largely because of Chile's political history. 'For so many years we were under a military regime with a very directive way of governing. As a result, society has fallen into this rigid, doctrinaire way of thinking. If you thought differently or began to ask questions, you ran risks.' They were risks which understandably few Chileans chose to take.

In a culture where life seems to have little meaning, 'young people come to the school groups because they know they will feel loved, accepted and valued.

'Moreover, whilst Santiago doesn't have the problem of shanty towns in the way that, for example, Lima does, most of our groups are on the edge of the city, where the children tend to live on a diet of bread and tea, and there are problems of malnutrition. School work makes demands on these children, and they don't have the energy to respond.'

'Children are made to feel worthless'

'There's also a poverty of stimulus. Most come from homes with a great many children in them. Father will be working, but earning very little. Mother will probably be working too, and often the children will be left alone at home, with just the TV going.

'They are made to feel worthless because of the words that are yelled at them or because they're beaten. They grow up with a huge problem of low self-esteem.

'Alfredo was growing up like this. His parents were separated, and he lived with his grandmother. He couldn't speak. He began to come to the SU group at his school. We began to talk with him and simply to repeat the message that he did matter, that God loved him and was with him.

'This took time. We go once a week to each group, and he was always the first there.

'After two years, his school work improved enormously and because of his testimony, a lot of kids have joined the group. And there are many like Alfredo.'

'Your life must not be wasted'

'We don't feel under any pressure to extract confessions from young people that they're sinners. What we are anxious to do is to show them who they are before God and the need they have of God. We go on to tell them about

Christ, but we begin by telling them that they are important, that God loves them and has a purpose for them. We tell them "Your life must not be wasted." And this consistent message has produced enormous changes.'

'Your life must not be wasted.' That's a message that young people in Chile need as much as young people everywhere else in the world. Thirty-nine percent of the present population of Chile is under twenty years of age. The majority are from poor social backgrounds. Many, whatever their background, feel there is no purpose in life and have a low estimate of their self-worth.

'The Roman Catholic Church has very little influence on our young people. Most of them are nominally Catholics because they have been baptised as Catholics. But by and large they have no commitment to the Church. They believe in God but regard him as very far away, and see no way in which that distance can be bridged. They think "God is so perfect. How could he possibly be interested in me?"'

Drugs, on the other hand, exercise a very powerful influence on the lives of many young Chileans. The use of cocaine in particular is on the increase. 'Our country,' says Paulina, 'has become a channel through which drugs are reaching the great markets of the world.'

'Alcohol is another way of escaping from reality, and in Chile it can be bought very cheaply.

'Young people are a challenge to us to present the gospel in such a way that they will give up these addictions.

'In their culture, it's their circle of friends who give them their identity. And when one person in the circle changes, the others make fun of them. So we need to link a new convert very quickly with a new group of friends.'

Eighty percent of first births to girls under fifteen

Another major feature of Chilean youth culture, says Paulina, is 'irresponsible sex'.

In Chile, eighty percent of first births are to girls under the age of fifteen. And most of the girls have become pregnant as a result of relationships with classmates at school.

The Chilean government has now passed a decree allowing teenagers who have had children back into the education system. And there was a 'huge scandal' when one political party started campaigning to distribute condoms to adolescents.

Meanwhile, says Paulina, there is total silence on the subject from evangelical churches, as if sex did not exist. Yet it is very common in these churches for youngsters to have to get married because of pregnancy.

So it's not surprising that sex education is one of the focuses of SU's schools ministry. As Paulina comments, 'It's really an uphill struggle in a society where the family has opted out of this area of life. And many teachers see abortion as the obvious answer.'

'We share our own story of our sexuality'

How do school groups respond when the Christian view of sex is presented? 'Many groups have laughed openly. But others have really listened. We go as a team of men and women, and when we share our own story of our sexuality, we've found that our testimonies have a tremendous impact.'

In one group, Paulina recalls, a boy stood up and said to one of our volunteers, 'Listen, I really want to know why you Christians say "No" to sex outside marriage. Are you married?'

So the volunteer said, 'No.' And the boy asked, 'Have you ever had sex?' And the volunteer again said, 'No.' So the boy said, 'Why haven't you?', and the volunteer was able to speak very freely about it.

How easy does Paulina find it to give her own testimony about her sexuality? 'I find it really hard, because you're sharing the most intimate part of yourself. And teenagers can see right through you.

'Before we share our testimonies, we begin by saying that we are Christians and that we believe that God made us and that we are therefore worthy of respect. Our life has a purpose and this has to be discovered. God has made us the way we are for our good – and this applies to our sexuality.

'We use the Bible as backup. The kind of way we use it depends on the group.'

Paulina, her widowed mother and one of her sisters share the family home in a middle-class area thirty minutes' journey from the centre of Santiago. 'I've always lived there. Our neighbours are families we've known for a long time.

'In my spare time I escape from Santiago and the smog that envelops the city almost all the year round. I go to the beach. It's an hour and a half's drive away.'

He saw Christians were 'anything but boring'

Paulina never rebelled against her family background, but she is sensitive to the needs of those who have. She tells the story of a boy with a Christian mother. He didn't want to go on studying and gave up going to church. 'He was tired of the traditional patterns of life and was in serious conflict with the authorities.' But he was persuaded rather against his will to go to a Scripture Union camp.

'He arrived in a bad humour. He was sure he would be bored. But little by little he became interested in the recreational activities and in the discussions. He began to realise that here Christians were anything but boring.

'When the camp was over, his mother was surprised at the way God had spoken to her son.'

No, Paulina has never rebelled against the faith of her parents. But she feels as strongly about the hypocrisy of some Christians as she did when she was a teenager. She finds she is annoyed by the inconsistencies between what they preach and what they practise, by Christians who lack integrity and also by those who lack social sensitivity.

'I try to see how God has had mercy on me'

Rightly she looks for high standards in SU staff and volunteers – for a depth of commitment, a determination to get down to the job, a willingness to be trained and to listen to what God wants them to do.

Yet she acknowledges that the Lord has led her from a kind of perfectionism to a more gracious and sympathetic attitude, particularly with young people.

'We need to recognise that we're not perfect. All of us are travelling on a journey, and our model is Jesus. He knows what it is to be human and can pray to the Father for us and for the Holy Spirit to fill us so that we can live in a more disciplined way.'

And when sometimes she finds it difficult to cope with failings in other Christians, she says, 'I always try to look at myself and see how God has had mercy on me – and I know that I must do the same with those around me.'

'I HEARD THE GENTLE WHISPER OF GOD'

Lydia Trnkova

CZECH REPUBLIC

'I don't feel good enough to be written about!' That was Lydia Trnkova's first reaction when I asked if her story could be part of this book.

Lydia lives in Prague, a city she loves. 'It's a beautiful city, full of religious history.' She is Scripture Union's first staff member in the Czech Republic and on that she comments, 'God called me. I never thought this could happen in my life. I take it as a miracle.'

Father held five years in a concentration camp

Lydia's family have lived and suffered through the turbulent history of their country this century.

Her grandfather was killed in the First World War.

Her father, who was his eldest son, was a very caring person who grew up with a keen sense of responsibility for his widowed mother and the rest of the family. He was a bookseller and during the Second World War he became involved in the Czech underground movement against the Nazis. He was arrested and spent five years in a concentration camp.

When he was released in 1945, he went looking for his mother, only to find that she had been killed by a bomb in Prague during one of the last air raids of the war.

He met his wife-to-be at the church they both attended.

They married and had two daughters, Lydia arriving some eighteen months after her sister Marta, who has always been very close to her.

Lydia has happy memories of her childhood in a Christian family. Her father has influenced her very deeply. His terrible experiences during the war had made him even more sensitive to the suffering of others. His health had been damaged whilst he was in the concentration camp, but 'he never complained. He remained a cheerful Christian.'

'When he died, I struggled...'

'We were very poor,' Lydia recalls. 'There was no bathroom in our flat, and the toilet was outside along the corridor. My mother often wished for a nicer flat, and my father could have asked the officials for one, because the Communist president of our country had also been in the same concentration camp.

'But my father wouldn't do this. He always said that if the powers-that-be had given him a better flat, "it would have meant doing something for them in return."'

He died of cancer when Lydia was fourteen. 'My father had a strong faith, and I felt very secure while he was alive. But when he died, I struggled. I felt very lonely. Teenagers need security.

'I had never doubted that there was a God. But I really lacked security in my life. I felt very much alone.'

'I saw I had to give my whole self to God'

'One day I was reading my Bible and came to a verse which spoke to my heart. It was Malachi 3.10: "Bring the whole tithe into the storehouse, that there may be food in my house. Test me in this," says the Lord Almighty, "and see if I will not throw open the floodgates of heaven and pour out so much blessing that you will not have room enough for it."

'I saw that I had to give my whole self to God and then I could test him. How strange that God himself with all his majesty and authority invites us to test him!

'I made that step of surrender. I prayed that I would give to the Lord all of my life, all my feelings, all my circumstances...

'He gave me wonderful peace. I haven't had that peace all the time since then, but I have always known he is caring for me. And in every time of doubt or difficulty, I remember his wonderful promise to throw open the floodgates.

'That step of commitment that I took was the beginning of a real relationship with God.'

In the Communist years, fear and faith

But Lydia took that step in Czechoslovakia while the Communists were in power. How difficult was it for her in those years?

'As a child, I was very much afraid that others would know that I was a Christian. There were teachers at school who could be very cruel. I was afraid that one of them would ask "Who is a Christian in this class?" I knew I wouldn't put my hand up. But I always knew that at home I could feel free to be myself.

'When I was older and had fully committed my life to Christ, I never tried to hide what I believed. People would see that I was different. They knew the reason and would even respect my faith.

'I remember that once a year at work we used to have a political talk from one of the leaders of the Communist party. He was obviously a dishonest man, and I was quite fearful about discussing my political attitudes with him.

'But when I was called into his room, he had just started to talk when the telephone rang, and he said "I'm sorry. It's urgent. I have to leave." And instead I found myself talking to a man who was one of the top people in the organisation, but couldn't be a director because he was a Christian. We had a very friendly talk. So once again I experienced God's presence and leading and loving care.

'I worked for the Foreign Trade Corporation and when I went on a business trip to Moscow, I took a few Russian New Testaments with me. It was very difficult to get Bibles and New Testaments through the borders, but I prayed and got them through. I had the great experience of the Lord leading me to a lady to whom I gave the New Testaments. We had a few minutes' prayer together. Both of us were in tears.

'I learnt during the Communist regime to rely on God.

'All Christian activities except church services were forbidden, but we organised camps for Sunday school children. Sometimes we had to tell the children to keep quiet so as not to attract attention, but God kept his hand over us.'

A teenager in the 'Prague Spring'

Lydia remembers the 'Prague Spring' of 1968, when Alexander Dubcek tried to introduce 'socialism with a human face'. 'It was a wonderful time, when the whole nation started to say what it thought.' Lydia was a teenager at the time and when she had finished school, she was able to go and stay in England for a few months. 'That was a great gift from God.

'It had always been my dream to visit England, and God made it possible. You see, Britain is in some ways culturally close to the Czech Republic. And God must have known already that he would need my knowledge of English for SU in my country. I met so many wonderful Christians in England. That will always stay in my memory as a very bright time in my life.'

But the Prague Spring, that time of freedom and hope, did not last long. 'The greatest shock was when the Russians came and occupied our country overnight. August 21, 1968 was a black day in our history.

'I was still in England, and in some ways it was even harder for me, because I could watch the fighting on television. I have always loved my country and that suffering made me love it even more.'

'It seemed hopeless. But God was in control'

'I came back to Prague in December 1968 to find posters on the streets saying "Soviet Union for ever". It seemed hopeless. But God was in control. The Prague Spring had brought changes for the better, but Communism had to collapse completely before a new thing could happen.'

Lydia comes from Bohemia. Jan, her husband, comes from Moravia and they met on 'neutral territory' in Slovakia at a youth camp. 'We were married quite soon.'

At one stage, four generations of Lydia's family were living in a five-room flat in Prague. They were next door to the broadcasting station that was the scene of the first fighting in 1968.

'My grandmother had one room. My mother had another room. Jan and I and our first child were in the third room, and my sister and her husband in the fourth room. We all shared the one kitchen. So we experienced what it means to be Christians in a family!

'Then my husband bought a piece of land and started to build a house himself. So our son didn't see much of his father because after he had finished work, he would go and get on with the building. But now we are so grateful to have a lovely house with a garden.'

Energies spent on survival

'In the Communist era, most of our energies were spent on survival. We'd be in long queues for food. But we never lost hope, even if the situation seemed hopeless.

'Once we invited one of our daughter's classmates to Sunday school. She was so excited and brought her sister with her as well, even though it meant an awkward journey by public transport. We gave them Bibles.

'Then something happened at our daughter's school – we don't know exactly what – and she became very afraid. She closed up within herself and lost her self-confidence. She's fifteen now and still remembers that time with tears.

'In those days, there was a deep longing for freedom in our hearts. We didn't know God's plan.'

'I could talk about the Velvet Revolution for hours and hours'

'But then came the great miracle, the Velvet Revolution, on November 17, 1989. It's five years ago now, but it's still so deep in my heart that it seems as if it happened only last month. It's so precious to us.

'I can remember how excited we were. There were demonstrations in Wenceslas Square, and Vaclav Havel would be speaking. My husband and I went there every day. There was such a wonderful feeling of unity. People became so kind to each other. It was such a joy. There was snow, but people didn't feel the cold.'

And now, years later, the wonder of that miracle is still with Lydia and her family. 'Sometimes something is said about God on TV. For example, the Minister of Education made a speech and said "I wish you God's blessing". It's so moving to hear God's name mentioned in public. Always the tears come to my eyes.

'I could talk about this miracle for hours and hours.'

Even before these momentous events, and while the Communists were still in power, Scripture Union in England had been in touch with Lydia. With her help, English staff had run training courses in Czechoslovakia for Sunday school teachers – in secret. 'We laugh as we look back on it now, but in those days we were afraid when foreigners came. It was dangerous to be seen talking to them.'

After the Velvet Revolution, Lydia was invited to SU conferences outside her own country. 'The atmosphere was so wonderful. I really felt in heaven. I'd never experienced anything like that.'

Back in Prague, there was a shortage of English teachers, and Lydia found herself teaching in a school. 'That was extraordinary. During the Communist regime no Christian was allowed to teach!'

Lydia became more closely involved in Scripture Union's ministry. 'I have always taken God's word as a precious thing. I could therefore identify with SU's vision of bringing people closer to God through the Scriptures, and I had a vision for SU in my own country.'

So Lydia was appointed as SU's first part-time (!) staff member in the Czech Republic. She didn't realise how the work would grow!

Pioneering publishing venture

Her own church had been using SU's *Learning Together* materials in English for some years, and she thought how marvellous it would be if other Czech Sunday school teachers, who didn't know the English language, could use the materials, too. So she began work on translating them.

To publish her translation was a pioneering venture with all the usual risks. How many people would buy it? What would they think of it? The Czech economy was in transition, and it wasn't easy to find a printer. When Lydia had found one and he had done his work, there was the laborious process of distribution. Lydia's husband and children helped, and her mother too.

They hadn't had much time to advertise, but at the first seminar at which it was introduced, they sold two hundred copies. Sales climbed up to a total of a thousand – a significant number for a pioneering venture in a comparatively small country. And people didn't just buy the material. Many said how much they appreciated it.

And the first ever SU camp...

Lydia also pioneered the first SU camp for young people in what was then Czechoslovakia. That wasn't easy either.

It was hard to find the right venue. 'Finally God opened up the way for us to discover a building in a beautiful village in the mountains north of Prague. It wasn't luxurious, but there was a big hall belonging to the house, where the students could play games.'

She sent out invitations to young people in the churches. Any of us who have ever sent out invitations to some brave new event know what it's like. You wait for the response with a mixture of faith, fear, doubt and hope.

'Lord, send me some applications tomorrow'

Lydia had very little response to her invitations. So little that she prayed, 'O Lord, is this camp really your will?' Then she asked God for something very specific. She said, 'Please, Lord, if you want this camp to go ahead, send me some applications tomorrow.'

So it was with some suspense and excitement that she waited for the next day's post.

She found God had answered her very specific prayer. That next day, a few letters arrived. And they were followed by many more. Every place was taken. So, as she said when telling this story to the delegates at SU's 1992 International Conference, 'I had to ask God to stop it!'

A party of young people and leaders travelled from Britain by minibus to share in the camp, and the Czech teenagers were able to have an English lesson every morning. Crafts and games were on the programme, too. When the Christian message was shared each evening, 'It was wonderful to see how the young people listened and responded in their hearts, and how they grew spiritually.

'One of the girls at the 1992 camp (the one that nearly never happened) didn't want to have anything to do with God. But she couldn't go on like that, and the Lord spoke to her so clearly that she gave her life to him.

'It's a joy to see how the Lord is changing the lives of young people. They're very dear people. I love them so much. I thank God for them.'

'Only Jesus can heal those hurts'

What aspect of the Good News is particularly attractive to young people in the Czech Republic? 'I believe that God speaks to each person in a different way. But many young people have been hurt in their lives, and some of those hurts are still causing pain.

'The only person who can heal those hurts is Jesus. He is so loving and such a friend that he understands perfectly every hurt in our lives. He alone can give freedom from those hurts. He alone can give us meaning and purpose.

'We saw this after the Velvet Revolution. Statistics showed that people – and not only young people – were interested in Christianity because of forty years of emptiness, in which there was nothing on offer to give them fulfilment. But now lots of evil things have come into our country, and we Christians need to be aware of that.'

'Reading books is in my blood'

Christians are human, and those who pioneer new ventures for God are no exception. Lydia confesses that she loves ice cream. And potato salad with pork. And a special Czech dish called *svickova*, which is a kind of gravy made of vegetables served with beef and dumplings.

'And I love reading books. I have it in my blood.' She is, remember, a bookseller's daughter. 'It's a great luxury when I can sit and read – and very relaxing for me. I hope that in heaven there will be lots of books to read!

'My husband Jan also likes books, and we both enjoy classical music and going to concerts. We're fond of the Czech composers Dvorak and Smetana, and their music says a lot about our country.

'Ours is a small nation, and we like to travel beyond its borders and see new things. We can go anywhere now, but it's still very expensive. I hope we'll be able to travel before we're too old.'

But of course Lydia's humanity extends far beyond a love of music, travel, books and ice cream.

'God spoke to me through the story of Elijah'

'My work for SU is very demanding. I had reached a point where I felt too exhausted to fulfil my first responsibility under God, which is to my family.

'Then God spoke to me through the story of Elijah running away to Horeb (1 Kings 19). Like Elijah, I heard the gentle whisper of God saying, "Go back the way you came." I was very encouraged by that.

'And God spoke to me through what I was translating, through the story of Gideon, who felt so small. Our task is to follow what God has prepared for us.

'In so many ways God is showing his blessing to me and to my family. I'm so grateful that my seventeen-year-old son Jan has been able to visit England. Our elder daughter Martina has done well in her exam. She says "God helped me". And our younger daughter has had a good first year at school. God is really showing us his blessing and his love.'

'I'M A HUMAN BEING AS WELL'

Andy Saunders

ENGLAND

Andy Saunders is a Londoner and proud of it.

He grew up in Highams Park in north-east London, and his bedroom had a red carpet. That, according to Andy, is the main reason he supports Arsenal, one of England's 'Big Five' football clubs, and in the opinion of Andy, and a few others, the biggest and best of them all. For red is Arsenal's colour.

Andy has twin brothers who are three years younger than he is. One of them is a policeman, and the other works in a clothes shop in Walthamstow market, not far from the family home.

'Mum was a churchgoer. So all three of us went along to the local Methodist church. My brothers opted out, but I didn't. The church had a very good youth group.'

Made his way down the aisle to the front

In July 1978, when Andy was sixteen, he went with the youth group to hear Dave Wilkerson of *The Cross and the Switchblade* fame speak at a meeting at Westminster Central Hall, opposite London's Houses of Parliament. At the end of the meeting Dave Wilkerson appealed to young people in the audience to go forward to commit their lives to Christ.

That was a moment Andy will never forget. 'My head was saying "You go to church. You don't need to make a commitment." But my heart was really pacing. It was as if it was wanting to go down the aisle itself.'

But Andy's heart didn't have to go forward alone. For Andy himself – head, heart and all – made his way down the aisle to the front. 'I made a stand that night – and I've still got a photocopy of the programme.'

It was his life at school – Sir George Monoux's School in Walthamstow – that changed dramatically as a result of his commitment to Christ. 'When I went back to school, they noticed that I had stopped swearing and telling dirty jokes and smoking. At school I'd been known as "Smoky Joe". That was my nickname.'

In fact, he didn't stay at school much longer. 'At sixteen, I'd had enough.' So, with some O-level qualifications as proof of his ability, he joined the staff of Midland Bank International in the City of London.

'Mum used to work in the City. I was there myself for five and a half years – and I still miss it. I miss the people. I miss working with non-Christians. I enjoyed working in teams.

'There's a buzz about working in the City,' says Andy, and there speaks a true Londoner. But he confesses that in his last two years with the bank, he was 'fed up with just pushing money around'.

An apprenticeship – buying the canned drinks

Meanwhile, his gifts with young people and in evangelism were being noticed. He served a very useful apprenticeship with Waltham Forest Youth For Christ. Initially, he helped with their catering. 'No, I didn't do any cooking. I used to buy the canned drinks and the cakes and the crisps. And then I would sometimes be asked to give my testimony.'

Thus far, Andy had been working with leaders whom he knew well, and he found a degree of security in that. But then he was invited by Steve and Rita Redding to join the team who were running the Scripture Union holiday beach mission at East Runton on the Norfolk coast.

Andy admits, 'I nearly pulled out. I was scared! Instead

of being with youth leaders I knew, I would be with a team I'd never met before. It would just be me and God.

'But once I'd got over the first two or three days, I was OK. The teamwork was good. The young people we were working with appreciated the fact that we were there. And when I looked back over the two weeks, I could see how God had used me. I'd survived it and enjoyed it. The weather had been good and I'd made some really good friends.'

Gradually, Andy's life was changing direction.

He gave his employers in the City six months' notice. He started work as a short-term volunteer with a Christian organisation, and then a Trust in the USA offered to pay his fees for a two-year course at Moorlands College, a theological training college, and off to Moorlands he went.

During college vacations he worked regularly in the mortgage department of a leading insurance company. 'They even gave me free lunches!' And as Andy the City banker became Andy the 'full-time' Christian worker, his parents were very supportive.

'I walked round the City in a daze'

The end of Andy's course at Moorlands coincided with the departure from the college of Stuart Pascall, who had headed their Department of Evangelism. Whereupon the college invited Andy to help with the practical side of their evangelism training, particularly until Stuart's successor could be appointed.

To say that Andy was surprised is an understatement. 'I was gobsmacked. They'd offered me a job! I was working temporarily in London at the time, and for three days I walked round the City in a daze.'

To switch at Moorlands from student to staff member wasn't easy. 'All my relationships had to change because of my change of role.'

'A very small fish in a very big pond'

What above all else had Andy learned from his student days at Moorlands? 'That I'm a very small fish in a very big pond. That was a hard lesson for me to learn and a very humbling one.

'Now, when people say "You're an evangelist", I say "I'm a human being as well. I make mistakes." '

Andy stayed on for a second year in his training role at Moorlands College to help the newly-appointed Head of the Department of Evangelism, David Edwins.

Now it so happened that David had been the Scripture Union evangelist for Wiltshire, Dorset, Hampshire and the Isle of Wight. And during his time at Moorlands, Andy had become a seasoned SU volunteer, particularly at the children's activities at that biggest of all UK Christian events, Spring Harvest. 'So Cathie Smith, who was then SU's Head of Missions, encouraged me to go for Dave Edwins' job.' Which Andy did. He got the job and so joined SU England's team of twelve staff evangelists.

'I miss London'

Has it been difficult for a true Londoner like Andy to get used to living and working as an evangelist so many miles from the Arsenal football ground?

'Yes. I miss London. Everything's there. There are so many different cultures. Everything's going on around you. There's the noise and the smell.

'The pace of life here is slower. The needs of the people are less obvious. They're more hidden. But I don't think people are more difficult to relate to, though some of them have had trouble with my east London accent.'

Andy, like Dave Edwins before him, is engaged largely in church-based evangelism amongst children, young people and families. Does the fact that his is a church-based ministry mean that he has a cushy job?

'We're up against the major problem that children, young people and adults say they believe in God – but don't understand the church. So we have to encourage churches to work in the community. We've got to go out and get to know our neighbours and respond to social needs – such as those of one-parent families and the unemployed.'

'Jesus sat and listened'

'I'm finding more and more that you've got to say to people "I appreciate you and accept you for who you are."

'You have to earn the right to share Jesus.

'Jesus sat and listened to people and that's what we need to do more and more.'

But, though churches may not be understood, and may not always be user-friendly, and may not always listen as they should, the advantages of evangelism being church-based are plain and clear. 'When I move on, the church will still be there to follow up and to nurture and care for the people we have contacted.'

They're reluctant to accept Christianity as the only way

Andy certainly doesn't stay within church walls. His ministry takes him into schools, and he finds that it's the exclusive claim of Christianity to be the only way that young people at school are most reluctant to accept.

When he is communicating the Good News of Jesus to children of junior age, what is his starting point? 'Jesus as a friend. That's where I always start. Friendship is vital in everybody's life. I tell them Jesus wants to be their friend.

'Sin is not a word they understand, though they know they do things that are wrong.

'If you say "Saviour and Lord" to a child, what does it mean? But from the age of five or six, they can have a good understanding of who Jesus is and why he came and why he died and they can apply it to their own lives.'

How would Andy answer the person who says that you can't talk to juniors about the cross because they would find it too frightening?

'See what they watch on TV! . . . I don't dwell on the gory side, but I have shown scenes of the crucifixion, and five year olds can take this if you prepare them carefully and tell their leaders what you're going to do.'

Kids from lone-parent families

But how much can children understand of the significance of the cross? 'I say that Jesus is my friend, and I always share with them that friends of Jesus go to heaven to be with him when they die. That's sufficient. If they ask me, I say that other people won't.'

Children don't grow up in isolation. They belong to families of assorted kinds. 'A high proportion of kids we contact, especially in schools, come from lone-parent families, or from homes where one parent is not the original parent.

'When I say "your family" to children, I always go on to say "They're the people who look after you at home". I never say "your mums and dads at home". I say "The grown-ups who look after you". For many of these kids, it won't be mum and dad.'

For a typical church-based mission, Andy will book the dates a year ahead, and he will prepare not only by meeting and training the church's volunteer team of helpers but also by visiting local schools.

When the time comes for the event itself, Andy generally reckons to arrive at the church on a Monday to set up his equipment. The mission (usually called a holiday club) will then run from the Tuesday to the following Sunday. There will be five mornings of activities for the seven to twelve age group, some afternoon events for younger children, a youth evening, an all-age family event on the Friday or Saturday night and a family service on the Sunday morning.

Obviously this kind of programme is only possible during school holidays and at half-terms. However, a number of churches run more limited programmes over a week during term-time, holding the meetings after school each day.

'I share Jesus as naturally as...'

'My aim,' says Andy, 'is always to enable the church to carry on after I've gone and to integrate the holiday club into the normal life of the church. I also aim to give training to the volunteer helpers and to help the church to be better known in the community.'

And is his aim evangelistic? 'I go for the drip, drip approach. I share Jesus as naturally as I would share a TV character like Edd the Duck. All through the week, in the quizzes, the craft work, the parachute games, Jesus will pop up naturally. They know that throughout the week they can come up and ask questions and there are counselling booklets that they can take.

'I believe that children should be encouraged to make their decision to follow Christ in their own time and in their own way.'

'Success is when children come back...'

'Recently,' said Andy, 'someone asked me "What's your success rate?" So I said, "That's an interesting question..."'

Andy believes that 'the success of any event is when children come back the next day.

'Success is when a kid at the end of the week has had a positive experience of what Christianity is about. Success can also be that kid making a decision for Jesus the following week.

'But success can be a volunteer team member who feels more skilled.

'I'm not into the numbers game.'

'A positive experience of what Christianity is about' – that's what Andy aims to give children in the schools that he visits as part of the preparation for the mission. He asks the local church to make contact with the school and he goes in 'to share the Christian faith and to promote the event'.

Some answers are difficult to argue with

But Andy doesn't need to go into a school to get unorthodox answers to his questions. In one church-based mission, 'after we'd watched a video on Jesus healing the deaf man, I asked the children why Jesus had done this. They gave a variety of answers, and then one child said, "It was his job!" I couldn't argue with that!'

Beach missions still have advantages

August finds Andy at the Cornish seaside resort of Bude, leading one of the beach missions that have been part of SU's evangelistic outreach since way back in 1868.

The beach mission idea has been transplanted to the sunnier shores of Australia, New Zealand and South Africa – and more recently across the North Sea to Germany. But is an idea that was dreamt up on Llandudno beach in Victorian Britain still relevant after more than 120 years?

Andy believes that beach missions still have many advantages, and he spells them out. 'You work with a team. You present the Christian faith in a public place, though I admit that people don't stop and watch in the way they used to. But holidaymakers are more relaxed, so they feel freer to share their problems with you. You can build up friendships over the period of the mission.'

Sharing traumatic experiences

As relationships are built up in the sunshine and rain of an English summer, confidences are shared. 'Young adults have told me about traumatic experiences – rape, abuse and all sorts of grim family situations. They've shared how worthless they feel as a result of these experiences.

'One girl told me how guilty she felt because she'd been raped three years earlier. All the guilt had been put on her by the guy.

'Young people have told me some horrific things. They only do that when they know I'm prepared to sit and listen and won't come up with glib answers. And this only happens when I'm prepared to share my own life and to share that I've been through tough times.'

Andy is back on a familiar theme. 'Jesus listened, and we need to listen.'

But are there hazards that go with Andy's job as a professional evangelist?

'Yes, you work on your own a lot, and that makes it

very different from working in the City or being a student. Often there's just you and Radio 4.

'What's more, if I don't have a faith, I don't have a job. So I have to make sure that my Christian faith isn't based on the fact that I must keep a job.

'But God has called me to share my faith.'

Evangelist with a taste for Sunday roast

Andy's favourite meals are roast dinners with parsnips and cauliflower. And when he goes back home to his parents in his beloved London, 'I find my favourite meals appear on the table.'

Andy the evangelist is a human being with a taste for Sunday roast. But a girl in a school once said to him accusingly, 'You don't live the real world. You became a Christian too soon.'

To which Andy replied, 'I still jump up and down when the mortgage rate drops.

'Being a Christian doesn't mean you can go around on cloud nine. You still have tough times. Getting that across seems to reassure so many people.'

In fact, Andy believes that what young people find so attractive about the gospel is that Jesus isn't just a historical character. He's alive – and the Christian faith can be lived out in the real world.

'So I talk about why I became a Christian. About tough times at the bank. And I share that I have a hope that I base my life on.

'I'm quite happy to wait for heaven. But part of the Christian calling is to pull heaven down to earth.'

As Andy reflects on what it will mean for him to go on fulfilling that calling, he wisely ponders the question, 'How will I change so as to stay relevant? I want to keep going until I retire.'

'To see him fired up for God...'

Meanwhile, there are encouragements on the way. Andy was with an SU group at a conference centre where two other groups were staying. 'On the day I arrived, I walked past a guy and thought I recognised him. Then it clicked! This guy had become a Christian on a house party the previous year where I had been the chaplain. He had since done his A-levels and was now taking a year out to be a volunteer worker at a church before going on to university.

'He had come to that house party with many questions about the Christian faith, and over the week they were slowly answered. To see him a year later fired up for God, and being used by him, was such an encouragement.'

Andy is convinced that 'as the next ten years go by, we will see people making stronger commitments at the start of their Christian lives, because they will have thought through the issues more deeply.'

That's why Andy says, 'I have a lot more hope than I had ten years ago.'

'WE'VE NEVER MISSED OUT ON ANYTHING'

Daniel Agopian

FRANCE

'I can remember my father coming back from a hard day's work. I could hear him whistling Christian choruses in the street. There were hardly any cars in Aix-en-Provence in those days. The small town, with its eighteenth-century buildings, was like a village. People would talk across the street from window to window, and you could smell the cooking in other people's houses.'

Daniel Agopian has very clear memories of Aix, the town near Marseilles in southern France where he was born. 'I left Aix when I was eight years old, and I resented that a lot.'

'With only their shirts on their backs'

He was an only child in a close-knit family. He remembers that on Sundays they used to go on a round of visits to see uncles and aunts and grandparents.

All four of his grandparents had escaped to France from Armenia in 1926 'with only their shirts on their backs'. At that time, many Armenians had been massacred by the Turks, and many of their children had been brought up in orphanages. 'My two grandmothers were brought up in American Christian orphanages in Turkey.'

The family background was not only Armenian but also Christian. 'The Armenian tradition is strongly rooted in church life.

'One of my grandmothers always had a Bible close at hand. She was always saying "thank you" to the Lord, even for small things. We used to feel that this was a bit exaggerated. But now I'm so much more aware of all the small everyday things that we owe to God.'

One of Daniel's grandfathers was a miner. It was the only work he could get. But he had a very bad accident, falling forty metres down the pit, and 'because there were younger children to provide for, my father at the age of fourteen had to take his place in the mine, and he worked there for five years. There were two older children in the family – one was studying theology, the other was in the French Resistance.

'Later my father married, and he and my mother were very active in our church. At the same time, after my father had done an exhausting day's work, he would go to the local theological school in the evenings to train to be a pastor. He did that for six years.'

He needed to 'belong' somewhere

'That's why we left Aix when I was eight years old. My father had finished his training, and we moved to a small town in the foothills of the beautiful Cevennes mountains, where he pastored a church. The town was in a mining area in the southern part of the Massif Central, 100 kilometres north of the Mediterranean coast.'

Daniel resented that move, and it became his ambition to pass all his exams quickly so that he could get back to his beloved Aix and go to the university there. Although both his parents had been born in Marseilles, he was keenly aware of the lack of roots in his family. He felt he needed to 'belong' somewhere. That's why he loved Aix so dearly.

But meanwhile, the church in the Cevennes was very much alive – and it gave him, as an only child, lots of friends.

'My coming to Christ was a gradual process. I was always aware that God existed. But when I was about thirteen, I gave my life to him at a youth camp organised by our church. I realised that I needed to be forgiven.

'I went on with God all through my teenage years. And during my time at university' (yes, he did succeed in getting back to Aix). 'I was engaged in all sorts of church and evangelistic activities back home at weekends.'

Daniel made steady progress as a Christian – except when he went to England. He took a one-year appointment at Bath University as Lector in French, 'something in between a lecturer and a student'. With so many fine buildings dating back two hundred years, Bath reminded him of Aix, except that 'it was much more posh.'

A catastrophic first date, but...

'I had an easy but an empty life there. I had a lot of money and free time, and a lot of friends who were not Christians.

'But I met an English girl, Gill. She was studying French, though she wasn't in one of my groups. I was reassured to discover that she was the daughter of a minister. I'm not sure if it was "love at first sight", and I was very shy with her. But I decided that before I went back to France at the end of the year I would invite her out anyway.

'That first date was a catastrophe.

'The next time I saw her was back in France one year later. Gill had come to Aix University for a year as part of her language course, and (by the Lord's coincidence!) we met up again. This time our friendship developed. We realised that God had not allowed our relationship to begin in England at a time when, for various reasons, we had both excluded the Lord from our everyday lives.

'But now we came to the point where we had to take a decision. I was going out to New Caledonia in the South Pacific for two years' voluntary service – as an alternative to one year's compulsory military service. So Gill and I had to choose either to get married – or else to separate for two years. We chose to get married, and the time of preparation for our wedding was a time of deepening our relationship with God.'

Not exactly a honeymoon

'We went out to New Caledonia to help, but we were helped a lot ourselves in return.

'It wasn't exactly a honeymoon. Despite the natural beauty, tropical climate and magnificent landscapes, it was quite a hard life. We were helping to start a new work.

'We also realised at this time how much of our culture we Western Christians add to the gospel when we go overseas.

'People in New Caledonia would take Holy Communion with cooked yams and coconut milk instead of bread and wine. They had a very different relationship to money. Culturally speaking, they are much closer to Bible times.

'This was a period of revival in my Christian life – and in my life in general. Particularly as a result of reading a number of Christian books, I felt much more filled with the Lord's love for people. I was very aware that the Lord who loved me was with me at every moment of my life. Also I was more open to other people. And I had a greater desire to read the Bible. So this culture shock was very good for me!'

Daniel and Gill stayed in New Caledonia for five years, teaching in schools run by the local evangelical church.

Move to minus fifteen

But then God called Daniel and Gill to move to a very different climate. SU France needed an administrator. Daniel accepted that call, and in January 1983 they left New Caledonia, with the thermometer at thirty-five degrees celsius – to arrive in snow-covered Guebwiller, then the headquarters of SU France, with the temperature at minus fifteen!

What's more, the long, cold winters at Guebwiller in north-east France were a far cry from the balmy ones that Daniel had known in Aix and the Cevennes in the south, where it was not uncommon to eat meals outside in a sheltered spot at Christmas or New Year.

For Daniel it was more than a change of climate. It was

a change to a very different kind of job. He had studied economics as well as political science at university and he had taught it – 'but teaching it and practising it are two very different things.'

What's more, within a few months, and before they had even finished unpacking their boxes, SU's General Director in France suggested that they should move again.

He'd only gone halfway

The movement had just embarked on a £1,600,000 project to build a new conference centre at Rimlishof. There was a need for someone to take charge of every aspect of this project.

Daniel's and Gill's first reaction to this suggestion was to say 'No' to another move. 'But one day,' as Daniel recalls, 'the Lord showed us very clearly that we should say "Yes". I was reading a book by Watchman Nee, and he explained how, when Abraham had set out from Ur to go to Canaan, he had stopped in between at Haran, and the Lord had had to show him that he had only gone halfway.'

So they accepted this second call and moved a few more kilometres to Rimlishof to live at the new centre.

Any project like Rimlishof inevitably has its problems. Daniel hadn't been trained to do the job he was now doing, so he found the problems more difficult to handle. But he looks back on his time there as a time of personal growth. 'I'm grateful to the Lord for having used me in his work at Rimlishof.'

The original vision was that Rimlishof would just be a centre for SU camps during the school holidays. So the accommodation and the furnishings were somewhat basic.

But Daniel felt it would be a pity if the centre were to be closed for most of the year. 'When I arrived, I realised that my vision for the project didn't correspond with the vision of my colleagues in SU. It wasn't that they were against what I envisaged. It just hadn't occurred to them.'

Daniel's vision for Rimlishof was that it would be not only a holiday centre for SU camps but also a year-round conference and training centre for SU and the churches around. 'I wasn't very interested in being just a conference centre manager, but I was ready to do the job in order to achieve this aim. And this was the direction in which the Lord seemed to be guiding us.'

A vision fulfilled

So, little by little, Daniel saw his vision for Rimlishof fulfilled. He was able to add furnishings and facilities, so that it became a centre that was admirably suitable not only for children and teenagers in the holidays but also for adults used to a more comfortable lifestyle – and for all seasons.

He initiated a Bible-based training programme, and his background in economics spurred him to train and encourage Christians not to withdraw from public life but to be salt and light in a non-Christian world. 'We had some big guns leading these training courses at Rimlishof.'

In 1988 Daniel made it known to his colleagues that he was ready for a change of role and that he felt that Rimlishof needed new leadership. 'I had been a technician. The need now at Rimlishof was for a pastor who could preach and train.'

At around the same time, SU France had a new General Director, and he had taken on the job on the understanding that he would have an administrator to share the work with him. So in August 1989 Daniel and Gill and their family left Rimlishof to move back to Guebwiller, and four years later, when SU France's national office was relocated in Valence in the Rhone valley, the Agopians moved into a house in a village nearby.

'We are so grateful to God for a house of our own. Our experience is that since we responded to God's call to full-time work, we've never missed out on anything.'

Their four children now range in ages from fifteen to seven, and in their village they have more opportunity to mix with other children than in the Rimlishof days.

Aware that the children of 'full-time' workers...

Daniel is keenly aware that the children of 'full-time' Christian workers can feel a bit neglected. They may sometimes think they don't come very high on their parents' list of priorities. 'I want our children to realise that I want to work full time for God. But I don't want to come home completely harassed, and I don't want them to feel that they are unimportant compared with working for God. It's a difficult balance.'

Daniel works what is a typical French office day – from 8 am to 12 noon and from 2 pm to 6 pm – plus extra time, for he often finishes much later and brings home work at night. 'When the children are coming home for lunch, I come home for lunch, too. And I try to be back in the evenings before they go to bed.

'Gill and I don't go to a lot of church midweek meetings, but we do take part in a group for couples who really want to share practical experiences from their everyday lives as Christian parents and citizens. This is a very encouraging group.'

Daniel enjoys 'walking around the mountains'. He likes helping his son with his model-making. He's an enthusiast for black-and-white photography. And he enjoys eating *saucissons* – a sort of dry French sausage – 'and a good Camembert, washed down with an earthy red wine'.

'I am a man of the night. That's when I read the Bible.'

He's an emphatic believer in the importance of the discipline of a special, daily time with God. He usually has a prayer time in the morning: 'I want to tell God how much I'm relying on him. I want him to direct my life, my work.

'But I am a man of the night, and that's when I read the Bible, when my brain is working much better. I take time to meditate. I think back over the day, perhaps in relation to the verses of the Bible that I have been reading. If I don't have this time of meditation, I feel something is missing.'

'We meet a lot of disappointed people'

Daniel believes that, for good or ill, France and other Latin countries are slower than America and Britain to adopt the latest trends in culture and fashion.

On the other hand, he believes that 'you Anglo-Saxons are more practical in the way you present the gospel. In France we tend to be more abstract.

'We meet a lot of people who have been disappointed by the Roman Catholic faith. When we speak to these people about God or Jesus, we're not on the same wavelength at all, because they have a distorted view of God. They associate him with blackmail. Some priests encourage this: "Do as we say (but not as we do) and you will be saved. Otherwise. . . ."

'Protestants are a very small minority group here in France. But they also include people who have been disappointed by what they have seen or heard in churches. Many of them want to know more about God, but not in a church . . .

'We in SU France are well aware of all this, and we try to be very concrete and specific in the way we present the gospel to those who have never gone (or no longer go) near a church. At the same time, we endeavour to help the churches in their ministries.'

'I like organising'

Daniel's own ministry in SU is to set others free to make God's Good News known, others who have gifts in teaching and evangelism. He does this by exercising his own God-given gifts in administration and finance, areas of activity that so many 'full-time' Christian workers find irksome and unappealing.

'I like organising. I like working with other people. It's so rewarding when you see Christians from different backgrounds and different churches working together, and the Lord has unified us. That's a good testimony to the world outside.

'I like it when representatives come to the office to sell us things. Often they ask what we do, and very often we have good talks about God and the Bible, and I haven't been the one to start the conversation.'

Yet Daniel acknowledges that his is 'a hidden ministry, and sometimes it's hard to realise that behind all the figures and the finance is the gospel.'

'I love people who want to be salt in the community'

Who, I asked Daniel, are his favourite Bible characters? His reply: 'Joseph, David and Daniel'. And why? 'They were men of prayer, rooted in God and relying on God. At the same time, they were not afraid to get deeply involved in public life and in government.'

Says Daniel Agopian, 'I love people who don't want to be like monks but who want to be like salt in the community. We need many Christians who can be involved in business, in economics and in politics as children of God.'

Joseph, David and Daniel (the Old Testament one) . . . I suspect that they, too, might have said 'I like organising . . .'

THE GIFT OF LAUGHTER

Renate Franz

GERMANY

It seems as if Renate Franz is always laughing. And she doesn't laugh quietly.

Laughter has a key place in Renate's ministry as one of SU's children's evangelists in Germany.

I asked her if she'd been laughing all her life. 'Naturally,' she said.

But did it make a difference to her laughter when she became a Christian at the age of thirteen? 'I came from a non-Christian home. By mistake I took part in a Christian camp and that was just right for me!

'I'd had a very good childhood. I'd heard about God, but it had gone in one ear and out of the other.'

'I knew Jesus wanted me'

'At this camp, one girl told us that when she got forgiveness, there was great joy in her heart. I couldn't understand about forgiveness. That was a strange word to me, because I didn't think I was a sinner. Not me! But when she said she could jump up and down for joy, I thought "That's what I need!" There were many starting points that led to my conversion to Christ, but that was the most important one.

'I gave my life to Jesus. It is interesting to note that I didn't understand the gospel as such, but I knew Jesus wanted me.'

So how much do children need to know when they come to know Jesus? 'The most important thing to say to them is "Jesus loves you". Children don't know this. I didn't know this. Of course, there is much more to know, but this is enough for the first step.

'In Scripture Union we believe that conversion is sometimes a point in someone's life and sometimes a process. In my own life, there was a big point, but the process went on.'

More reasons to laugh – but not afraid to cry

Renate says that before she became a Christian, 'I had only looked for fun.' When she came to know Jesus, she found more reasons to laugh. But she also found that she wasn't afraid to cry sometimes.

In her pre-Christian days, she'd kept what we Brits call a stiff upper lip. To quote a German proverb, '(American) Indians don't cry.' But now that Renate had a friend who could help her, she found there was a place in her life for tears as well as laughter.

Renate became an SU volunteer in 1970 – partly through going on an SU skiing camp. 'I'm a passionate skiing fan.' She joined the SU staff in 1980. She's an enthusiastic leader of beach missions, and looks on them as one of the best ways of reaching people you would never find in church.

And there are certainly a great many of those! Church attendance figures published in 1993 show that in Germany as a whole, six percent claim to go to church regularly, thirty percent to go sometimes and thirty-two percent to go rarely. The percentages for the West are seven percent, thirty-four percent and thirty-seven percent, and the corresponding figures for East Germany are three percent, fourteen percent and fourteen percent.

About half the children Renate and her teams meet on the beaches in West Germany go to Sunday school or something similar. 'At the beach we have a mixture of Protestants and Catholics. And Catholics sometimes find our preaching of the gospel less difficult than Protestants.'

'I only come for that song!'

As elsewhere in the Western world, many tend to regard the pursuit of pleasure as their main aim in life, and Renate finds that this attitude rubs off even on children from Christian families – and on some of the helpers in her mission teams.

It is in this context that 'the daily 45-minute children's programme at our beach missions starts with some funny songs. Then we present the Bible story, in drama, mime or straight storytelling, trying to involve the children as much as possible ... Children who are interested and can read stay behind for Bible reading.'

'We sing one song during our children's programme in which all the children have to raise their hands and shout "Yeh!" One day I noticed that there was a very old man sitting in the front row. I said to him afterwards "You were enjoying that!" And he said, "I only come for that song!" We had a very good conversation after that.

'The children like their programme so much that many of them turn up half an hour before we start. It's thrilling to see how enthusiastic they are.'

'Many Christians live on a special island'

'We always end the programme with a word game which has no deeper meaning except that the children like it and parents see that Christians are "normal" people.'

So do people in Germany think that Christians aren't normal? 'Yes, because often they aren't!' says Renate. 'I think many Christians have a special island – they live on it and don't see what's happening around them. I often meet Christians like this. Christians need to be natural.'

It's certainly natural and normal for Renate to get a crowd of children to help her to tell the story of the yogurt cow and Jim, who belongs to a tribe who have only one word in their language, and that's 'Hahaganunu'.

Says Renate, 'We practise the word "Hahaganunu" with the children several times. They say it in a high-pitched voice, a low-pitched voice ... and so on.

'Now the story begins: Jim sits in his tent. He sighs:

"Hahaganunu!" (Every time the children join in.) That means: "I fancy strawberry jam yogurt." Jim gets up and opens his tent. He meets his sister, who asks in a high-pitched voice: "Hahaganunu?" That means: "Where are you going?" He answers "Hahaganunu?" That means: "I'm going to get some strawberry yogurt!"

'His little sister doesn't like strawberry yogurt and screams in a horrified voice; "Hahaganunu!" That means: "I can't stand strawberry yogurt!" Jim nods and says regretfully, "Hahaganunu." That means: "You don't know what's good for you!" And so the story goes on until Jim can finally milk the cow, singing a "Hahaganunu" melody with the children.'

Positive attitudes

And so the laughter of Renate's team and of the children is heard on the sandy beaches of Germany's North Sea coast. Nor are there too many scenic attractions to compete for families' attention. 'The only excitement' – apart from what Renate and the mission teams provide – 'is to play in the sand.'

SU's beach missions – totalling thirty or more each summer – usually last a fortnight, though some are shorter.

'The attitudes of parents is usually positive. They're happy for their children to attend the meetings because they realise how much they enjoy them. Occasionally we have long talks with parents, trying to answer their questions about God, Christian education and so on.

'I remember one woman who came to the programme because of her daughter. But as she listened to the gospel, she started thinking about Christianity herself. Some time after the mission ended, she phoned me because she had so many questions. I encouraged her to start reading the Bible. She found a church, which she still attends, and she has become a Christian.'

Rich people are polite but reserved

'Rarely at beach missions are we ever confronted with rejection, though now and then we have discussions with people who ask "Is there a God?" or who comment that "Every religion is a way to God" or ask "Why are Christians so intolerant when there are many ways to God?"'

But 'we are no longer going to islands like Juist, where the wealthy go, because working there became more and more difficult. Rich people are very polite, but very reserved. They have a "don't come too near me" attitude.'

It does sometimes rain on German beaches. When this happens, the meetings are held in a nearby building by permission of the local authorities. And 'if it's fine but windy, we try to get some shelter by arranging wicker beach chairs as windbreaks.'

Renate leads missions with the help of a team of volunteers, some of whom don't find it easy to make the necessary adjustments to their lifestyle.

'They have to eat the food we give them and to live with other people in a caravan in much less space than they have at home, and some of them find this hard. But I encourage them by saying "It's a new experience for you!" I try to help them to see the funny side of it and not to take everything too seriously.'

Starting where Paul did in Athens

I asked Renate, 'Where do you start when you share the gospel?' Her reply: 'I find the best instructions are given in Acts 17, in the report of what Paul said in Athens.

'Paul referred to what his audience knew and understood. He preached the great deeds of God.

'I don't tell the children all this in one meeting. But I tell them of the great deeds of God – how God in his love created the earth and the human race, how he sent his Son the stories of Jesus and how he was given for us...'

Renate emphasises that when she invites children to apply what they have heard to their own lives, she is careful to do so 'without manipulation or pushing'.

'Very few children at a beach mission commit their lives to Jesus there and then. But often in children who come to our meetings for years, we observe a long process of growing in faith.

'I told her that first of all she would need to have a close relationship with Jesus, that she would have to trust him. And she answered, "Oh yes, you mean I would have to be a Christian? I am a Christian." '

A cheeky, freckled four year old

When Renate and her colleagues lead children's weeks organised by local churches or run camps, they often meet up again with children they came to know on the beach.

'I well remember a four-year-old, red-headed, freckled, cheeky little nuisance. In our meetings on the beach, we taught the children the song, "God's love is so wonderful... so deep, so high, so wide." Suddenly the boy raised his hand and said, "God is so big and we are so small. And that God loves us!"

'About six years later, that same boy took part in a children's week in my native town. He asked me, "Do you remember me?" We could continue our talk together where we had off on the beach six years before.'

Away from the coast, Renate leads children's weeks in churches for most of the rest of the year. 'Most of the children who come are those who already know. But that doesn't necessarily mean that they do what they know!'

'Is it a circus tent?'

Two or three times each year she leads missions in a tent just six metres in diameter.

Who puts the tent up? 'We and the children do,' says Renate with a laugh. 'It goes up in a village or near a school or in a big city. If the children put it up, it's their tent, their place, they have a home inside. But they always ask, "Is it a circus tent?"

'A tent is neutral ground. You get a lot of children there who don't know anything about Christianity. If I start to pray, some of the children will look around and wonder what's happening. So I have to explain.'

One group of children were asked what 'Amen' meant, and a five year old said 'Goodbye'.

Each tent meeting ends with Bible study in small

groups, led by workers from local churches. Renate briefs them beforehand: 'You need to talk to the kids and make friendships. Get their addresses, invite them to your home and try to meet their parents. You'll still be here when the mission is over and I've moved on.'

How many children can squeeze into a tent about six metres in diameter? Apparently the record is 120. And what happens when it rains? 'The children still come,' Renate assured me. 'But the rain is very loud inside the tent. So sometimes all we can do is to sing. But we're trained to adapt to changing situations!'

Thinking and re-thinking how to present the gospel

In sunshine and in rain, Renate's aim is 'to make God and Jesus known in whatever way possible'. This, she emphasises, means 'thinking and re-thinking how to present the gospel in a way that people understand.

'Like a waiter I want to "serve" others in a loving, kind, "appetising" and enthusiastic way, to let them know what God offers and to win people for Jesus, so that they may become "satisfied". This is what I want. How this is going to happen is something I have to think about again and again. And I pray to Jesus for good ideas.

'The gospel is conveyed most strongly in the way we (helpers and full-time workers) treat the children. By our loving acceptance, we can help the children to begin to understand how God loves them.'

'Most children don't know Jesus loves them'

In Renate's opinion, the aspects of our multi-faceted gospel that appeal most strongly to the children she meets are that 'I am accepted the way I am' and that 'I am precious and loved'. And she would say again, 'Most children don't know that Jesus loves them.'

Renate lives in Frankfurt, where she and her widowed mother have separate flats in the family home. She enjoys food (especially meat and all kinds of salad), travel, music and photography. She likes being with people, but confesses she also enjoys being on her own in her flat, especially after a camp or a mission.

Though she believes that some Christians aren't normal, she herself most certainly is! But when you ask her whether being a full-time evangelist has meant sacrifices, she confesses to a different kind of abnormality.

'The greatest sacrifice for me,' she says, 'is not being able to live a "normal" life.'

'All the sacrifices worthwhile'

'Celibacy to me is no sacrifice. To me it's not something terrible but relieving and delightful. To some people that may sound strange, but being single gives you the opportunity to work in a way you couldn't if you were married.

'But I travel a lot. Most of the time I'm together with lots of people, and I'm hardly ever really at home. "For this world is not our home" (Heb.13:14), is what I'm trying to get to grips with at present. Sometimes it's a burden to pack yet again. But I like driving, and once I'm on my way, normally I'm fine!

'Sometimes I miss not being able to have regular fellowship with people at my church. I can't attend the meetings in the way that other people can. But then I think of the joy that my work gives me. I like travelling around, meeting people I didn't know before, and telling people the gospel – which is as relevant in the present as it was in the past and will be in the future.

'I'm looking forward to heaven'

What for Renate is the most satisfying part of her ministry? 'When people get to know Jesus better and are full of joy because of the gospel.' And the most frustrating part? 'You hardly ever see the results of your "work". It's mostly sowing in hope. That's why I'm looking forward to heaven.'

Meanwhile, laughter is part of Renate's survival kit. 'With a smile,' she says with a laugh in her voice, 'it's easier to survive, especially when times are rough.'

WHERE SLAVERY'S LEGACY LINGERS

Gene Denham

JAMAICA

Gene Denham grew up in a ghetto area in Jamaica. As she recalls, 'Policemen didn't go there alone, they went there in battalions.'

Her parents were not married to each other. She is her mother's eldest girl and her father's third child.

Her mother had four children. So did her father. 'So I have seven siblings. My father was married twice, but never to my mother. I don't come from a traditional European type of family!'

One of family of five living in one room

'I grew up with my mother until I was nine years old, and then with innumerable aunties, and with my father and his wife at some point. I had quite a mobile history, but it's very fascinating the way God takes what could have been a disadvantage and turns it into an asset. My own experience of the psychological pain of that kind of uncertainty – and the feeling of not belonging anywhere – has helped me to understand other people's pain.'

For most of her childhood, Gene lived with her mother and her mother's three other children in one room. Her mother used to wash and iron clothes for people who lived in the wealthier part of the town and Gene often used to carry the clothes back to the big houses in what seemed like a different world.

'God gifted me very early in life with a social awareness and a social conscience.'

Gene also recalls that 'there was a gentleman who lived in the same yard as we did. He was a follower of Marcus Garvey, who was a black radical leader in the 1920s and 30s. Looking back now, I can see that this neighbour of ours influenced me very deeply.'

Moved into a different world

Gene herself moved into a different world when she won a scholarship to Montego Bay High School. Later she transferred to St Andrew High School in Kingston, known as one of the best high schools in Jamaica – a typical English-style girls' boarding school. The boarders even had tea at 4 pm!

It was there, during her fifth year, that she became a committed Christian and began to grow spiritually, largely through the influence of the Inter-School Christian Fellowship group in the school. That was in 1966, when she was sixteen. 'Part of my struggle in my teenage years was about my identity as a black woman who had adopted a faith that was for the most part being presented as a white man's religion. It seemed to many that I was compromising my cultural integrity. My older brother, who is a Rastafarian, felt this very keenly.'

'I was going to be consciously black'

At high school, says Gene, 'I was even more acutely conscious of differences in skin tone. In our Caribbean culture, the saying goes:-

"If you're white, you're all right,
 If you're brown, stick around,
 If you're black, stand back."

'This was even more evident in the 60s. If you had black hair that was naturally curly, you felt it needed to be straightened. Many girls would iron their hair with a hot iron.

'That was the first shackle I threw off. It was 1968. I

said, "Never again." I was an Afro-Jamaican and I decided that I was going to be consciously black. My hair is natural and I wear no make-up.

'Since then, I have affirmed blackness as a vital part of my historic identity.'

'I share deeply the feelings of black Jamaicans'

'It's not very usual for a committed, Bible-believing Christian to speak the way I speak. But my willingness to explore what it means to be black has given me opportunities to talk with lots of black-conscious people.

'I share deeply the feelings of black Jamaicans. There is an intrinsic sense of worthlessness amongst us black people.

'Recently here in Jamaica I know of a little child, four years of age, who cried because somebody called her black.'

Such is the long-lingering legacy of slavery in Jamaica.

Here in Britain we think of slavery as an evil abolished by the Christian hero William Wilberforce, in period costume, in a bygone century. And so it was. Why then does its grim legacy linger on in the Caribbean? Why amongst so many young Jamaicans are there such feelings of helplessness and aggressive despair?

Gene Denham reminds us that Jamaicans were slaves for nearly 350 years – from the 1520s until the final break up of slavery in Jamaica in 1870, more than forty years after its formal abolition. During those three and a half centuries, the experience of slavery became part of the racial memory.

'Every aspect of our lives was organised by the powers that be to remind us that we were not really human beings, we were not really people. Everything black, negro, African was seen in a negative light.'

What slavery did to the black family

'Legal marriage was seen by the slaves as something that white people did.

'I don't think people in countries that were involved in

slavery understand what it did to the black family. When slaves came from Africa, they didn't come in families. Slave dealers made sure that families were separated.

'When they reached the Caribbean, one of the roles of the black male slave was to make sure he bred healthy slaves. That was the kind of relationship that existed between male and female. The black man never had a chance to feel like a man and protect and care for his family, so the black woman became the nurturer. There is a book with the apt title, *My Mother Who Fathered Me*.

'When slavery was abolished, the physical chains were removed far more easily than the psychological and spiritual chains.

'Even when Jamaica gained independence in 1962, society still looked up to white structures. And to this day black people have a hard time accepting anything that is black in a positive way – at least, as in the case of reggae, until the white world accepts it!'

'I don't have to feel inferior, I'm a child of God'

'My experience of Jesus Christ has helped me to look at the world and its complexity from a different vantage point. I don't have to feel inferior to anybody, because I am a child of God. And since the black experience in history has bred inferiority, that is Good News indeed.'

After high school, Gene went to Bible school, parttime. Then she studied full time for a degree in theology and also studied social work at the University of the West Indies. And, with a scholarship from the Billy Graham organisation, she went on to Wheaton College in America to study for her master's degree in counselling psychology.

'My opportunity to study in the States and to move around in black and white America helped me to enter even more fully into the feelings of black people. I have tried to let my Christian faith speak deeply and biblically to those feelings. I don't at all see the black person as always a victim. We are fallen, too.

'My faith must be part of my racial experience and vice versa. Jesus must be brought into everything without compromising the gospel and the plain statements of Scripture.

'I have tried desperately hard to understand the society in which I live and to see how the gospel to which I am totally committed relates to the racial and sociological problems of my country.'

Her own social background is more relevant than ever

Why and how did Gene Denham become a schools worker with ISCF in Jamaica eighteen years ago? 'Apart from the sovereignty of God,' says Gene, 'it was because I had been so influenced by our ISCF group during my last two years at high school.'

Today Gene finds that her own social background as a young person growing up in a poor community with a working-class parent is even more relevant in her schools work than it was when she began back in 1973. 'All that the travel brochures say about Jamaica is true,' Gene assured me. But she points out that Jamaica also has an unemployment rate that is nearly forty percent – and a high teenage pregnancy rate.

The overwhelming majority of Jamaica's population of 2.3 million are really poor. There is a dwindling middle class. Most people work as farmers or as small traders. The houses where Jamaicans live range from constructions made of wattle and daub or shanty-style cardboard and zinc to palatial residences which are the equal of any in the richer nations of the world.

Most heads of households are women. Men tend to be very mobile, and many have more than one partner.

'Still feeling the lash of a kind of slavery'

Education is modelled on the English system, but both health and education services are somewhat run-down and more and more teachers are leaving teaching. Many schools have had to put in a welfare programme and to give breakfast at school to kids who haven't been given any at home. But Gene points out that many pupils are too proud to eat a school breakfast even though they're hungry.

Back in the 60s, as Gene recalls, 'Education was regarded as a right for poor youngsters like me. Also, my parents were very helpful. They saw education as a means of getting ahead.' Today for many youngsters education is seen more as a privilege than as a right. 'Nobody don't care about us' – that expresses how most people feel. 'In this situation,' says Gene, 'the historical experiences of black people, though not easily verbalised, are even more keenly felt. The mass of Jamaicans are still feeling the lash of a kind of slavery.'

A 'turn these stones into bread' mentality

Understandably, money – sheer financial survival – is all-important to the present generation of parents. So they don't see much practical value in education, and many kids see no point in it at all. By contrast, drugs, and the money they can provide, are alluringly attractive.

Jamaica is said to have more churches per head of population than any other country in the world, but only thirty percent of its people regularly go to church. 'Only thirty percent,' emphasises Gene. And she adds that the witness of the churches is 'clouded by the economic survivalism that permeates our entire society. If something doesn't help to bring money in, it has no relevance. Sure, it's the same kind of "turn these stones into bread" mentality from Satan.

'This is compounded by the fact that our evangelical churches have not always seen how faith should inform lifestyle.' As elsewhere in the world, 'Some are schizophrenic in the way they live out their faith. They go in for the same crooked dealings as everyone else in order to survive...

'I don't have a great deal of confidence in our churches' ability to speak to the young Jamaicans. Young people are watching us adults in our churches, and copying the materialism that they see. We are going to be guilty of keeping them from the gospel because of our materialism.'

Gene emphasises that sharing the gospel with the young people of Jamaica is like sharing the gospel cross-culturally anywhere. 'The gospel transcends culture, but you need to know the culture.'

'The gospel must speak to their present experiences'

In the Caribbean, music – steel bands, reggae – is a vital part of the culture. 'The churches need to understand the place that music occupies in the lives of young people. Some churches still believe that anything that is not in four-four time is sin.

'The gospel has to be presented to the young people of Jamaica in terms that speak to their present experiences of alienation, hopelessness and despair. Jesus's humanity and divinity can speak powerfully to those themes.

'I am totally committed to Jesus Christ as Lord and Master. That is not negotiable at all wherever I am. I try to find out how the message of Jesus Christ can be presented so that young people can identify with it without compromising it in any way.

'You've got to find out first where people are. When I am witnessing and sharing with a young person, I first want to know whether they are churched or unchurched. They may well have a picture of church that's so negative that you have to erase a whole lot of wrong stereotypes before you can begin to speak the truth of the gospel. Many young people cannot handle or understand the drabness of their experience of church, and they throw out everything.

'You meet the young person who isn't able to cope any more with the advances of her father or her stepfather. You meet the boy who is living on the streets. He's stopped going to school because all his friends are on the streets. You meet the spoilt upper-class kid who doesn't go to church because on Sundays the whole family go off to their luxurious house on the north coast. Each situation merits an individual response and I try to be very aware of the person I'm speaking to.'

'I use the story of the rich fool a lot...'

'I'm a firm believer in John 4, in Jesus's interview with the woman of Samaria. I believe the Spirit of God helps us to be able to speak directly to individual young people. But I also think I've developed an awareness of the young people's world because that's where I've lived all my life, and that awareness helps me to speak directly.

'When I take devotions in a school, and speak to a lot of unchurched young people, I trust the Holy Spirit to lead me to biblical material that is relevant. I use the story of the rich fool a lot in devotions. I use the story of the woman of Samaria a lot. I use the Gospels a lot because the Gospels present a Christ who is very relevant to young people, though often they have never seen how relevant he is. For example, like most of them, he was obviously poor.

'Music has been so helpful in my ministry. I have recognised that kids like to see a guitar. I play an acoustic guitar. I like country and western a lot. Kids like it, too. I support the use of reggae as a medium for communicating words.

'My music gives me a hearing.'

'We watched her soften to the gospel'

For Gene there are many encouragements. 'I met a young lady named Glo at a camp. At high school she was very, very withdrawn and almost antisocial. For that reason she'd acquired an awful nickname. But at that camp we watched her soften to the gospel. Today Glo is a member of my church. She's actively involved in her college Christian Fellowship, and I'm so pleased to see how she's grown as a person and as a Christian.

'Helen Ann has begun a Christian home for street boys. We have had these boys at our camps. They were not used to authority of any kind. We watched them and in their own way they have grown so much through the Christian social levelling. They know they are accepted.

'There are not many kinds of young people that I have not reached, and the continuity of the work speaks to me magnificently of its relevance and its impact. We thank God for that.'

Not all success stories, but...

'It's exciting when people say to me "I became a Christian when you came to my school." '

But life for Gene is not all success stories. Roger, a teenager at a technical high school wrote to her and said: 'When my exams come round, I always end up failing. Gene, I don't know what to do. I pray, I curse myself, I hate myself and I try harder and still I am no better. I have always remembered what you told me that I must be a witness in my school work. I am confused. I don't understand. Why has God forsaken me...

'I have reached a point where I am thinking about suicide,' he continued. 'I know it's wrong, but what can I do?... What hurts me most of all is that the non-Christian students are doing better than me, and they tease me, saying, "You are a Christian, you know God and you are a dunce." Whenever they say these things to me, I want to break down and cry or jump off a tall building...'

But Roger asked Christians for help. He even shared his hurts and his depression with a hundred young people at an ISCF camp and, says Gene, 'You should have seen how the Holy Spirit used those kids to pray for Roger...'

In Jamaica, Scripture Union and the Inter-School Christian Fellowship merged in 1979. 'It's proved a good marriage,' says Gene. 'Scripture Union is a people movement and is sensitive to the needs of developing countries.'

The only possession she's really attached to...

Gene shares a house with two women friends. Each has her own room and they share the living room, kitchen and bathroom. There's a big yard space at the front and the back, and a large bougainvillaea at the front. 'I love plants and flowers,' says Gene, 'I wish I could spend more time tending them. They sometimes die on me.'

But the only possession she's really attached to is her guitar. 'I don't lend out my guitar. Your ministry tool is kind of special.'

One of her friends says of Gene, 'She lives simply. She's single-minded. And what stands out is that I've never seen her depressed about anything.'

'I'm not a Lone Ranger'

How would Gene herself describe her hobbies? 'I like being alone. I like to read, to go to the beach, to ride my bicycle, to visit friends, especially my godsons' families. I think kids are great, especially other people's kids, and especially if you can leave them and go home!'

And Gene's verdict on herself? 'I'm sort of a one-track person in many ways. I don't demand a lot from life, but I make demands on myself. I don't like laziness or indecision. I like sharing in ministry. I'm not a Lone Ranger.

'I find it difficult to get on with Christians who are wrapped up in their own little world and culture and know very little of what's going on in the rest of the world. Christians who think that their world is the only world that really exists. And Christians who can't see that to be different is not to be less, either in value, importance or significance.'

'I like Christians with a heart'

'I like Christians with a heart, Christians who are in touch with the world, who will ask me honest questions, Christians who can speak relevantly.'

'Let your heart feel compassion, let your eyes see despair,' wrote Gene in a song she calls 'Heart Dare'. 'For nearly twenty years now, I have sought to be single-minded in God's work.' No wonder she finds it hard to cope with Christians who don't look around, who feel no compassion and see no despair.

'I'VE FOUND JESUS'

Comfort Essien

NIGERIA

She still remembers the exact time she woke up. It was twenty to four in the morning...

Comfort Essien will never forget that night in the dormitory in her boarding school in Nigeria. It was the turning point in her life.

She was a fifth former at the time. She had been a Scripture Union member since she was in the first form and had become secretary of the school's SU group, but she found it difficult to recognise that she was a sinner. 'I did not see myself committing some of the more obvious sins, but there were times when I knew I fell short of Bible standards of Christianity.

'When my parents were praising me for being the best child in the family, somehow within me something would be saying that I was not as good as my parents thought. I knew I told lies, I was stubborn, I used to fight...'

'At lights out, I faced the fact that I was a sinner...'

But on that decisive night in the dormitory, as Comfort recalls, 'the whole fact of my condition before God became very disturbing to my mind. There was struggle going on within me. Just before lights out I reflected on the story of the Prodigal Son and this and other Scriptures became very vivid to me.

'At lights out I quietly knelt by my bed and faced the fact that I was a sinner, that I was wrong and that I needed God's forgiveness. And I invited the Lord Jesus into my heart.

'I must have prayed for over an hour without realising it. It seemed that I was away from the dormitory and in the real presence of God.

'Peace filled my heart. Before this, when I heard that somebody had died, fear would grip me. I thought, "Supposing you were that person, would you be prepared to face God?" ...'

'I was so excited that I ran ...'

'I had had a chest pain that the hospital could not diagnose. Doctors told me I would have to grow up with it.

'When I had prayed that prayer of repentance in the dormitory, I didn't ask God to heal me because I didn't know a miracle could happen. But that night after sleeping I woke up at twenty to four in the morning and found that the sickness had gone.

'I was so excited that I ran and knocked up the girl who was the president of the Scripture Union group to tell her my story. I shouted to her "I have found Jesus!"

'Next Sunday I had to share my testimony with the rest of the SU group in the school.'

That was twenty or so years ago. Today Comfort Essien coordinates Scripture Union's schools work in Nigeria. That means leading a team of around twenty staff members.

Dormitory floors are also for sweeping

She has written a booklet called 'Beginning and Continuing the Christian Life'. On the opening page, no doubt mindful of her own experience, she emphasises that you are not saved 'because you are a Scripture Union member or the secretary of your group ... Salvation is a result of your meeting with a person. That person is Jesus Christ, the Son of God, the Saviour of the world. Salvation is a result of accepting or inviting him into your heart ...'

'Actions speak louder than words,' says Comfort in the booklet's chapter on 'Witnessing'. 'Every piece of work that you do should show that you are certainly a child of God.' And here is one of the examples that she gives: Cleaning the blackboard should be taken seriously and done diligently, too – as to the Lord.'

Comfort firmly believes that dormitory floors are not only for kneeling on in prayer. They're also for sweeping.

SU groups in at least 4,000 secondary schools

With around twenty colleagues, it may seem that Comfort leads a sizeable staff team. But there are SU groups meeting regularly in at least 4,000 of Nigeria's secondary schools! (Even that figure doesn't include school groups in the north, where a sister organisation, the Fellowship of Christian Students, is responsible for the schools work.)

Yes, 'meeting regularly' – except when 'for the first time, teachers joined other workers in a nationwide strike, which lasted for months, and our schools work saw unequalled setbacks.' But over the years Comfort has had the thrill and the encouragement of working with young people whose stories have become similar to her own.

A teenager from Oluyole Estate Grammar School in Ibadan came from a deeply committed Christian family. 'In our home,' he said, 'one of the rules is that we must wake up by 5.30am daily for morning devotion and nobody must sleep until evening prayers are said.' Another was that, 'We must be in church before 9am for the Sunday school and morning services and by 5pm for the evening service.

'I grew up in this very disciplined moral religious atmosphere . . . I was vigorously involved in church activities, but this did not take away sins from my life. My belief then was that lying, stealing, fighting, anger, etc, were normal. While in the eyes of my church leaders and my parents I was one of the best boys, God knew me as one of the worst sinners.'

'The climax to my search'

'However, something gripped my heart whenever I did something wrong. I used to feel guilty, but this normally lasted for a very short while.' He was invited to some prayer meetings. 'In these meetings, and often with fasting, I desired to serve God better ... but I always failed.

'God sent one of my sisters to me at this crucial time. She introduced me to *Daily Power* (a booklet of SU Bible reading notes). I began to discover God in a new way when I started to study my Bible with the help of these notes.

'The climax to my search for salvation came when we went to an SU Easter Camp. On the first night the SU drama unit acted a drama entitled "Fragments of Hell", and I cried to God to save me from the lake of hell fire. There was joy and peace in my heart then, and the other parts of the camp programme – the Bible studies and the talks – reinforced my decision.

'Without follow-up my joy would have lasted for just a while after the camp. But God came to my aid and I was introduced to a Scripture Union youth centre that meets at 4pm every Saturday. The teachers took an extra interest in me and called me aside many times to encourage me, and because of their love and prayers I came to love Jesus and decided to live for his glory alone.'

Love and friendship vital in evangelism

To those of us who live in other cultures, this testimony and Comfort's own are a mixture of the familiar and the unfamiliar. To meet someone not yet committed to Christ who is genuinely God-fearing and in awe of judgment and the reality of hell would be to many of us a refreshingly new experience.

Yet there is so much in both testimonies with which we can all identify: the turning points which set our lives in a totally new direction; the excitement and joy of 'finding Jesus'; the value of a group with whom we can share our faith, and the love and the encouragement of friends.

'Oh! yes!' says Comfort, 'Love and friendship are vital

in evangelistic work with any group of people.

'Young people in Nigeria are burdened with various problems. A relationship of love and friendship enables them to unburden their hearts to those who minister to them – for counsel, prayer and possible practical help. The sensitive worker will be conscious of this need and ready to draw near.' It's no use just standing at a distance. 'In fact, many students look up to SU staff workers as their "mothers" or "daddies" . . .'

A surprising assortment of competing faiths

Thirty-seven percent of Nigeria's population claim to be Protestant Christians. As elsewhere in the world, many of these would be church adherents with no personal commitment to Christ. But nominal Christianity is by no means the only rival to the gospel with which Comfort and her colleagues have to contend.

A perhaps surprising assortment of faiths are competing for the hearts and minds of young Nigerians.

West of the Niger, Islam is biblical Christianity's main rival. Here, numbers attending school SU groups tend to be lower than in the east because of the Muslim influence. Yet Comfort is able to say that 'Muslims are coming to know the Lord Jesus, sometimes in a dramatic way.'

East of the Niger, where a typical SU group in a secondary school can number between 50 and 100 students, the main rival to the gospel is simple, straightforward materialism.

But there is sometimes an unholy alliance between materialism and nominal Christianity, resulting from so-called 'prosperity theology'. There are preachers in Nigeria (as in other parts of the world) who say that if a Christian is poor, that is a contradiction of God's word. And the poverty in the country makes this kind of theology very attractive to young Nigerians.

So how do Comfort and her colleagues cope with the subtle attractions of this teaching?

'We point students to Joseph, David and Daniel. We take them to the faith chapter, Hebrews 11. We show them that there are two groups of people in that chapter – those who were delivered from their problems, and those who were sustained in the midst of their problems but not delivered. There is a balance in the word of God.

'We point to Jesus as the supreme example. The cross is the symbol of suffering and of victory. There is no victory without suffering.'

As well as the subtleties of 'prosperity theology', says Comfort, 'some oriental mystical faiths such as Hare Krishna are gaining ground. The list of these is endless.'

Demonic forces – and subtle pressures

Comfort can never forget – while those in more secular cultures can easily forget – that she and her colleagues are engaged in a spiritual battle against the forces of darkness. In SU groups in Nigeria, says Comfort, 'there's a significant emphasis on prayer, because we're often dealing with students exposed to demonic forces, who need to be taught the importance of prayer and how to pray.'

Are there also more subtle pressures on young Nigerian Christians? 'There's been a great shift in recent years with increasing urbanisation,' says Comfort. 'Peer groups have gradually replaced parents as the major influence on young people.'

What about pressures at school on a committed Christian teenager? 'That depends on the inclination of the school authorities. If there is a Christian principal, Christian students may find themselves loaded with responsibilities because they are known to be reliable.'

Low marks – because they weren't willing to sell themselves

'But where the authorities are opposed to the Christian faith, because it touches them on sensitive issues, Christian students may be persecuted even to the point of expulsion.

'Some Christian girls have been victimised by male teachers. They've been given low marks so that they failed their exams, because they were not willing to sell themselves...'

To counsel young people in Nigerian schools can hardly be easy. So, 'When we appoint new schools workers,' says Comfort, 'we look for Christian maturity and balance, as well as for a deep sense of God's call, for a flair for schools work and a love for young people.' Like many other leaders, Comfort looks in others for qualities that she so obviously possesses herself.

Comfort lives in an SU staff flat, a three-bedroom apartment, with six younger relatives. And if you ask her about her own lifestyle and that of her colleagues, she is reluctant to say very much.

She just says 'We pray...'

However, she does point out that in Nigeria, teachers can't make ends meet on their salaries. When you question her about it, she tells you that SU's salary scale is much lower than the pay scale for teachers. And when you ask, 'So how do you survive?', she just says very graciously and uncomplainingly, 'We pray...'

It was during that memorable night in her school dormitory that her life changed direction. That new direction has never led her to material prosperity. Nor does she serve her Lord in a tranquil country. Her comment on the political turbulence in Nigeria is simply that 'Our God is on the throne. He will see us through.'

But in that dormitory at twenty to four in the morning, she shouted excitedly 'I've found Jesus'. And in the years that have followed she has had the joy and exhilaration of hearing many other young people echo those words.

'I TEND TO GRAVITATE TO THOSE WHO ARE FAILURES'

Joe Campbell

NORTHERN IRELAND

When he was only eleven years old, Joe Campbell felt a failure.

Joe grew up in what he describes as a 'very modest' middle-class, Presbyterian, churchgoing family in suburban Holywood to the east of Belfast. He has three sisters – two older and one younger than himself. 'We were a very happy family.'

But at the age of eleven, Joe failed an exam. That meant he couldn't go to the grammar school where most of his friends were going. What's more, he felt a failure at church, because somehow this was an exam that most churchgoing young people seemed to pass.

That episode has had a lasting impact on Joe's life. 'Even now,' he says, 'I tend to gravitate towards those who are failures in society rather than to those who are successes.'

Began as a messenger boy at fifteen

He left school at fifteen to work in the Belfast shipyard of Harland and Wolff. He began as a messenger boy. Then, when he was sixteen, he started his five-year engineering apprenticeship. He has happy memories of the shipyard. 'I learned a lot about life. I enjoyed the Belfast humour.' Joe rates very highly the ability of the people of Belfast to laugh at themselves.

It was at this time, too, that he acquired his love for competitive sailing, which is enjoyed by a wide cross-section of people in Ireland.

A long walk home to faith

He was working in the drawing office at the shipyard, and had begun to attend night classes. Then one Sunday evening, as he very clearly recalls, 'I came to faith in Christ through the Youth Fellowship at our church.'

He lived only ten to fifteen minutes' walk away from the church. 'But that night it took me half an hour to get home. God was speaking to me and doing things in my life. I was twenty-one, and when I got home I knelt down by my bed and asked Christ into my life. He came in and he has been true to all his promises ever since. There has never been a moment when I have felt that God has left me or let me down in any way.'

Joe was soon to make another discovery that was to mould the shape of his life. 'I began to do some youth outreach. And I discovered that I liked doing youth work, especially with young people who were not regular church attenders.

'This was in the 60s, and some local Christians were running a coffee bar called The Fishermen. It had nets and lifebelts and loud music and lots of swearing and smoking, and I warmed to sharing my faith in that atmosphere.'

Joe was given the opportunity to go on a teacher training course so that he could teach engineering skills.

A surprise – someone interrupted

He started teaching in Cairnmartin Secondary School in West Belfast. 'This was a revelation to me.'

Then, as now, many secondary schools in Northern Ireland had voluntary Scripture Union groups which met regularly. But when Joe went along to speak at his first SU meeting at Cairnmartin, he was in for a surprise.

'Someone interrupted my talk by asking a question.' Joe wasn't used to this. 'But I learned then that inner city young people do not sit quietly and listen to a religious talk. They want dialogue and action.'

So Joe and the other leaders of the school SU group adopted a different strategy. They saw that they could exercise their influence most effectively by taking parties of kids from the school away camping at weekends and on swimming and diving trips.

'When you share a tent with two or three young fellows in a rainy Northern Ireland summer, you no longer have a teacher/pupil style of relationship. And the powder for the milk gets mixed up with the powder for potato, and you're not quite sure what you're getting in the morning.

'I still see many of those lads, and some of them later became helpers at the YMCA. Several are now working with young people themselves.

'Cairnmartin is in the Protestant sector of West Belfast. Some of the kids were from broken homes because their fathers were in prison. There were young people in my classrooms who were using rubber bullets as erasers.'

From the foot of the mountains to the heart of Belfast

'I taught at Cairnmartin for two years, and then the school bought an Outdoor Centre at the foot of the legendary mountains of Mourn and I became its first warden. Pupils from Cairnmartin came to the centre for a week – twenty-five at a time – and at weekends lots of Christian groups came. And to this day SU and Crusader camps use the centre.'

In the summer holidays Joe went to the SU beach mission at the Northern Ireland seaside resort of Portrush. He was the mission's associate leader.

It was there that he met Janet, a nurse from London. 'She'd wanted to go to the Greystones mission down south, but the team was full. So she came to Portrush.

'After one of these missions, Janet went off to Peru with the Regions Beyond Missionary Union, but she caught hepatitis and after two years had to come home. She rejoined the Portrush team the following year, and we fell in love and married. We have three children. God has blessed us richly.'

Joe left the mountains of Mourn to work in the very heart of Belfast. He took on the awesome assignment of being Youth Director of the City of Belfast YMCA.

A new centre had just opened. The YMCA was and still is in the traditionally neutral ground in the middle of the city between Catholic West Belfast and the Protestant East. Joe was there for eleven years, working with both Roman Catholic and Protestant young people.

'The YM was an oasis for young people in a city of hatred and violence.

'We were very busy. Sometimes we had 300 young people a night, the vast majority with no church connection.'

Joe confesses that it was at the YM that he had his first real experience of Catholics. 'Previously I had had one Catholic friend, and that was all. And I had been taught that Catholics weren't Christians, and that to become Christians they needed to become Protestants.

'Now I began to see another side. There were some Catholic young people who came on to the leadership team at the YM, and we would pray and break bread together. A turning point came when I was being asked questions, and the answers I had been taught to give were no longer adequate.

'As a group, we made a journey together. Not only did we as leaders change, but we saw young people both Catholic and Protestant coming to faith in Christ.'

'Yes, we were caught up in the violence'

'We were able to give young people an experience of the Kingdom, and to help them to work for justice. There were times when we caught a glimpse of what might be.

'Outside the YM – especially late at night – there were constant fights, but inside there was respect for the other side. But yes, we were caught up in the violence. One of my co-leaders had to go to court and give evidence against one of our young people. She'd seen him beating up a

Catholic lad.

'Often we would be in court defending our young people because we could see positive aspects to their character.

'There was one lad whose mother was being treated for cancer and whose father was living in London. The lad himself had been unemployed for most of the previous three years. He tended to be violent, especially on Friday and Saturday nights when in the company of his mates.

'After I had represented him in court and gained him a much-reduced sentence, I showed him our monthly prayer calendar and how on that very day about sixty Christians throughout the city were praying for him, and he broke down in tears. He has since responded well to individual help.

'Sometimes we had violence inside the YM. Pool cues were broken over people's heads. It was heart-rending.'

Bomb scares – and young people coming to Christ

'There were constant bomb scares. Volunteers had their cars damaged or stolen at night. We used to have police "visits" – until we insisted that police were not allowed inside the building without a warrant. Police were welcome to have a cup of tea at the front door, but not to go inside. This was important, because to some of the Catholic young people the police were very bad news.

'It was often in one-to-one situations that young people came to faith in Christ. But we also worked hard at providing a centre spot in the evening's programme when something could be said on faith issues.

'We always gave young people plenty of choice. For example, they could watch cartoons or play table tennis or join a discussion group or a Bible group. They were never forced. But over the months people began to know where we stood on important issues – including new life in Jesus Christ.

'On one of our walls there was a rack where we put a host of leaflets on various topics, sexuality included. We always had some attractive gospel booklets there. Other leaflets were found on the floor. But you never found a copy of *Journey Into Life* or *The Way Ahead* on the floor. They just went missing, and were replaced. You sensed that there was a hunger and a thirst – and that the Holy Spirit was at work.

'As a team of leaders we always met before club for prayer for thirty to forty-five minutes, and these times of prayer were always open. Young people could come in and often they did. Frequently the first indication that God was doing a work in their lives was when they turned up early and a little embarrassed to sit in with a group of leaders and to pray. Young people would share. They would ask for prayer for a job or for a place to live in or for a family member who was seriously ill.

'I discovered that though many inner city young people don't have a faith of their own, they respect people of prayer. We made it clear that if we could do nothing else, we could pray.'

Friendships across the divide

'Young people, Catholic and Protestant, were together, and often friendships were formed across the sectarian divide.

'I remember having a phone call from a mother saying that her son was going out with a Catholic girl, and what was I going to do about it? I was subjected to several phone calls like that.

'And I remember a young Catholic fellow and a young Protestant girl. They'd been going out together for eighteen months. They were both working and they were mature young people. They wanted to get engaged. But their families wouldn't let them. The heartache and burden were often overwhelming!

'Sometimes, in situations like that, if they defied their parents and married, they had to live way outside the city in a neutral area. And sometimes they emigrated and the country lost them.'

'Some of our young people were killed'

'To me personally, these were times of learning but also times of great pain.

'Some of our young people were killed in sectarian violence. There was one young lad. He worked in the prison as a pay clerk and came to faith in Christ in our youth club. When he married a lovely Christian girl who also came to our youth club, many of the leadership team were at the wedding.'

Joe still cannot recall what happened three months after they were married without tears.

'They were both on their way to work in their car. She stopped the car. He got out to go to his job in the prison and she drove on to the insurance office where she worked.

'At 8.30am that morning I had a phone call to say that he had been shot dead. I had to go and pick up his wife and take her home. Some of our young people came to faith in Christ through that situation. It was a very painful time.

'There were other killings and some of the young people who were involved were part of our youth club and are now serving long sentences for murder.'

The unemployed as easy prey for the paramilitary

'In the early 80s, when unemployment began to hit really hard in Northern Ireland, we started to run training courses in the daytime for sixty or seventy young people. The unemployment rate in the Province was around twenty-six percent, but amongst young people in inner-city areas it was often as high as seventy-five percent.

'I'd gone to the shipyard as a fifteen year old and worked with men. I'd eaten my lunch with men old enough to be my father or my grandfather.

'Now generations of young people haven't had that experience, and they've not grown up, because they haven't had the opportunity to be treated as adults.

'These unemployed young people were an easy prey

for the paramilitary organisations, the IRA and the UVF. We were conscious that we were working with these young people and befriending them during the day, and they were responding to us – but that at night some of them had another life. Some of them were training in the junior wing of the IRA or the UVF. For a while, they would avoid capture. But then one day they just wouldn't turn up and their friends would tell us that they had been arrested.'

Came back – often direct from prison

'Part of our job was visiting them in prison and going to see their parents.

'They always came back to the YMCA – often direct from prison or the young offenders' centre, with their black binliners and all that they owned inside. They saw us as people who accepted them, and the YMCA was a place where they felt welcome and at home.'

How did all these experiences change Joe as a person?

He saw that the traditional evangelical emphasis on individual discipleship was inadequate. 'We quickly realised that if we were going to follow God in this situation, we had to follow God together. We were welded together as a team. We prayed together, we went on holiday together, we broke bread and shared wine together.

'We were a church. There was a sense of identity, and our whole attitude to violence and sectarianism was put into sharp focus.'

'We were wearing down...'

'We were seeing a side of life. But when we went to our churches on Sundays, they couldn't see it and didn't want to see it. For them, shutting out that other side of life was a defence mechanism.

'But it was difficult. As a team and as individuals, we were wearing down. My links with Frontier Youth Trust were very important to me at that time. I was on the Committee and then became Chairman of the FYT Committee in Northern Ireland, and that gave me the opportunity to visit other FYT regions. Those visits were therapeutic and refreshing. Now as an FYT Field Officer I try to provide similar opportunities for other youth workers under pressure. It's good to give people reasons to get out of their situations, even for a weekend.'

Joe was with the Belfast City YMCA for eleven years. Then, when he felt he'd given the best that he could, the way opened up through the Mennonite Church for him to go to the United States for a year, with his family, to study. When he returned home after a briskly stimulating time, the post of FYT Field Officer for Northern Ireland became vacant. Joe was the obvious choice and he joined the Scripture Union staff team.

Pastoral support for youth leaders under pressure

'I have three main roles. One is to give pastoral support to youth leaders, and especially to full-timers. I meet individually with ten or a dozen of them once a month for about one and a half hours, just to listen.

'Youth leaders are under tremendous pressure.'

'Many have risen above the hatred...'

'Christian youth leaders see life at the sharp end. They love Jesus Christ and want to see how their faith interacts with the issue of sectarianism which is ripping the Province apart. The old answers are no longer good enough.

'There was a girl who was literally burnt out of her home by hate-filled Protestants some years back. Her father died, her mother briefly remarried only to be widowed yet again.

'Though she was subject to times of severe depression, she became involved in a youth club leadership team. She came to a living faith in Christ after an FYT conference at Swanwick in Derbyshire. She is a gentle, caring girl who is beginning to mature in Christ.

'And there are many like her, brought up in streets of violence, who have risen above the hatred and found new life in Christ.

'Because of the constant high unemployment among young people in Northern Ireland, we're seeing a great proliferation of schemes and programmes, and Christians are finding their way into staffing these programmes. It's a way of reaching young people, and FYT provides support and training to enable them to cross the cultural divide.'

'Gospel gives hope in a hopeless situation'

What then, I asked Joe, is the Good News for the young people of Northern Ireland?

'I see the gospel as setting them free to be themselves, free from a sectarian upbringing, free to be the whole people that God wants them to be, free to be young. The gospel gives hope in a hopeless situation.

'We've had more than twenty years of violence. We keep thinking that next year ... or the next initiative ... will bring peace ...

'But many Christians in Northern Ireland feel very despondent. They feel maybe that God has failed or that their type of theology is a failure. Strangely, there are many churches in Northern Ireland which do not often pray for Northern Ireland, even if there's been violence two miles up the road.

'The gospel must give people hope. And if it is to be relevant in Northern Ireland, the gospel must be seen to break down the dividing wall of hostility between the two communities.

'One of the great sayings of Protestant people in Northern Ireland is "For God and Ulster". But what we have to say is "For God and God's glory alone". There will still be theological differences between Catholic and Protestant churches, but what unites us is far greater than what divides us.'

How does Joe explain to young people how to come to faith in Christ? And does he explain it differently to Protestants and to Catholics?

'I may use different words, but the central elements of

confession and acceptance of Christ will be the same. So I invite people to acknowledge that they're not good enough for God on their own and that they need the Saviour and, having acknowledged that, to recognise that Christ is the one who is good enough, and that he has stood and indeed hung on the cross in their place, and that he invites them to trust in him.

'That's a very simple message. But it's the message that needs to be heard.

'It does not mean that the young Catholic person will leave the Catholic Church. It means that they will stay there and work for change. They may need help from outside – maybe some kind of fellowship group – but many Protestant young people will need that kind of support too.'

'Words on their own are cheap'

'But the message for frontier young people is not just words. Words on their own are cheap. Young people need words in the context of a relationship with a person they trust.

'In our frontier youth work we need to work hard at building relationships of trust, so that young people understand the gospel not only with their ears but also with their hearts – and see it with their eyes.

'Many young people are at the very edge of society. They're feeling the brunt of injustice. And they want to see and hear about a Jesus who sides with them. There are lots of examples from Scripture of Jesus siding with the weak against the powerful.

'Many frontier young people see government and church and society over against them. We need to allow them to see the Jesus of the Gospels, who was not wedded to these institutions.'

'I like to unveil the revolutionary Jesus'

And is the message a message of reconciliation? 'We need to make it clear in our presentations that Jesus is not the possession of the Protestant or the Catholic community.

Scripture tells us that Jesus is beating a different drum and marching to a different step, and that both communities are out of step with him.

'I like to unveil the revolutionary Jesus in ways young people can understand. What does it mean in Northern Ireland today to "turn the other cheek", to "go the extra mile", to "love your enemies"?'

Joe's youth work experience has led him to ask these hard questions. Another hard question is 'When did the disciples become Christians?'

'Often in frontier youth work, you find young people who are almost ready for leadership, but they're not yet one in the faith with you, though they're not opposed to it. I believe we should try to bring young people like this on to our teams. Because I believe that many of Jesus's followers became disciples on their journey with him and not at the starting-point of their story in the Gospels.'

'Churches are often impatient'

Like many another youth worker, Joe finds that churches are often impatient about outreach to young people. 'We're not prepared for the long haul. We want instant results. Yet if we were sending missionaries overseas, we would allow them to work for ten or fifteen or even twenty years before expecting "results". So why not apply that same principle to those who are working on urban housing estates in this country?'

Joe and his wife Janet and their family Esther, Colin and Lisa live in a fifty-year-old house in the Belfast suburb of Holywood, where he grew up. Joe says that their house needed fifty years of repair when they first moved in.

'I do see signs of change in Northern Ireland, primarily among young people who are not following in the old footsteps. But I love gardening, and the gardener in me tells me that these tender green shoots will take time to grow, and will need nurturing and encouraging along . . .'

'Lights burning in the darkness'

'We have to work hard at loving our enemies, at not

allowing the bitterness and anger we naturally feel to take root. To go out of our way to foster relationships with the other side. Yes, it does take a deliberate mind set.

'Belfast is almost completely surrounded by hills, rather as the prophet described Jerusalem. There are many points where you can look down and out over the city at night.

'I am often reminded that there are individuals, small groups and whole churches working for change, justice and reconciliation, often at great cost, like lights burning in the darkness. It is my great privilege to meet increasing numbers of these people from both sides of the divide.

'Every single follower of Christ in Ireland has a role to play, however small, and we covet greatly the prayers of God's people throughout the world as we learn what it truly is to be God's people in a violent land.'

'I WAS STAGGERED THAT GOD HAD USED ME'

Janice Aiton

SCOTLAND

'I'm an Ayrshire lass. I was brought up in a loving, caring, understanding environment. I was encouraged to be myself and to be independent.'

Janice Aiton's father was an industrial relations officer in a steel works before he retired; her mother managed a jeweller's shop in Glasgow.

Her brother William is two years her junior. 'We were very close when we were younger. We enjoyed playing football, tennis, darts and particularly cycling together.' Her sister Aileen is eight years younger than her. 'As a teenager, I was very conscious of the age gap between us. It seems much less now, and we share an interest in ballet, theatre and the cinema.'

A question from a four year old

Janice's mother would go to church on special days such as Communion Sundays, and Janice was sent to Sunday school. She graduated to the Bible class and then to the youth fellowship. She enjoyed church activities and when she was sixteen, she began to help with the three to five year olds on Sunday mornings.

'At the time I was working at a local newsagents' on Saturdays and during the Easter and summer holidays. And I was invited to work on Sunday mornings.

'This happened as I was wrestling with the whole idea

of the Christian faith. I was questioning things. Then one Sunday morning a four year old asked me, did I know Jesus? Could I please tell him what he looked like?

'I realised that I didn't know Jesus, and I felt the time was right for me to leave church and to accept that offer of a Sunday morning job. So I did.

'But in fact my connection with church wasn't severed. I changed churches and went to one on the other side of town which had an evening service. My younger sister often came with me. My parents didn't encourage me in this. I went to this other church entirely of my own volition.'

'I still didn't really know Jesus'

'At Glasgow University I studied French, German and history. I still didn't really know Jesus, and my reading of Voltaire, Camus and Sartre was a challenge to the Christian belief I was beginning to grasp. But I realised that I was worshipping knowledge and that it is impossible to acquire all the knowledge that there is.

'I was aware of the greatness of God as the source of all knowledge and wisdom. This didn't draw me closer to him, but it sustained me and I kept up my churchgoing during my university days.'

She went on to a college of education to train to be a teacher. The college was a disappointment. She felt restricted, hemmed in, deprived of her independence. But she thoroughly enjoyed her teaching practice. 'I believed then that the biggest thing that I could give to young people was the developing of their minds. Now I realise that the greatest thing that I can give them is to open their hearts and minds to the Lord Jesus.'

Her first teaching job was a tough one. It was in a boys' independent school in Glasgow, and she was the only female full-time member of staff.

'Hard to hand over control, but . . .'

'Up to then I'd had two gods – self-sufficiency and independence. During that year God in his own way broke down both those gods and caused me to search more deeply and to look to him for help.

'My head of department was a Christian, and he influenced me greatly by his lifestyle and his approach to work and to people.

'I went to a Christian rally, and God spoke to me about the breaking of the Ten Commandments. I realised that I'd broken all ten of them in one way or another. I saw how Jesus Christ fitted into the scheme of things. I understood the miracle of Calvary, and realised that I needed Jesus.

'I'm such a strong-willed person that I found it difficult to hand over control of my life to someone else. But I saw that it was best to surrender everything to the Lord Jesus. I found that so hard, and I still find it hard. But I've never regretted that decision.'

'I refused three times'

'I'd never had any previous connection with Scripture Union. But twenty-five boys from our school were going to an SU camp and the leader showed up at school and invited me to join the camp team. I refused three times, but eventually I was coaxed into going. I went with a great deal of apprehension, but it was a terrific experience and it led me to a deeper involvement with the SU movement.

'I was conscious that God was leading me on from teaching, but I wasn't sure to what. I thought it might be parish ministry, and I had a year as a student assistant in a church, teaching, sometimes preaching – and visiting the bereaved and the elderly. I enjoyed the pastoral side, but I missed the dynamism and vitality of young people.

'I went to help at a national SU camp on the Isle of Arran. I shared a tent with an SU staff member, Morag Stenhouse. I was invited to speak on Jesus's words "I am the resurrection and the life", and God used me in a way I'd never felt before. Many youngsters were moved by the Spirit to acknowledge Jesus as their Saviour and Lord.

'If God wanted me, he'd open the doors'

'It seemed that God was saying that I should work with young people, and during the camp Morag asked me whether I'd ever thought of working for SU.

'I reckoned that if God wanted me to work for SU, he would open all the doors. I wouldn't push any. And it was a joy to see that happen.'

Janice is very far from being a loner. 'I like working with people.' But she confesses that she can find it difficult to get on with people who have a particularly negative outlook – and with those who have a very narrow and limited view of the role of women.

'Young people have never tried Christianity'

She's a schools worker in Scotland, and Scotland is certainly not England. It's another country with its own identity. Scottish young people have their own brand of humour, and Janice feels they may be more taciturn and therefore possibly more reluctant to share their faith than young people in some other countries.

But the big issues they face – sex, drugs, alcohol, peer pressure – are by no means peculiarly Scottish. Nor is Scotland the only country where the average teenager finds traditional church services unattractive – or would do if he or she were ever to attend one.'

'They may not hear of Jesus anywhere else'

'Jesus went into the synagogue. But he also went out to where the people were, and so must we.'

And unless they're ill or playing truant, where young people are is at school. There are Scripture Union groups in 700 Scottish schools, and over many years SU Scotland has built up a reputation for the quality of its schools work and its camps programme.

'I enjoy taking school assemblies,' says Janice. 'They're a captive audience. They may not hear of Jesus anywhere else.

'In primary schools, you can get real involvement. In

secondary schools, you must pitch what you say where young people are at.'

Most of the voluntary Christian groups in Scottish schools are called Scripture Union groups, and Janice defends the use of the name. 'Young people know exactly what they're coming to. They're not deceived or deluded. Yes, there'll be fun and laughter, but also a serious element, a focus around God's word.' Naturally, groups vary in size, and some are more outward looking than others.

School missions

Janice and her colleagues are also able to run school missions – taking assemblies and RE lessons and organising lunchtime and after-school activities. Some of the missions are on a larger scale; others target particular year groups. There can be drama and audio-visual presentations. They try to involve local churches, and follow-up is vital.

Does Janice feel at all nervous or apprehensive when she goes into a school? 'No, I usually feel quite at ease. I just love interacting with young people. I just love it. And I find that I have a good rapport with heads and with teachers. I still mark examination papers, so I keep my hand in educationally.'

'I love assault courses'

Each year, around 5,000 young people attend SU Scotland's camps. They're extensively advertised by the showing of slides in schools. SU has a high reputation 'for providing a safe, caring and loving environment. And the prices of our camps are so reasonable – that's part of their appeal.'

Janice is a bubblingly enthusiastic camp leader. 'I just love sport. I love abseiling, I love assault courses, I love football, I love ice-skating.'

She also confesses 'I enjoy leadership', though she admits that it can be slightly daunting to go to a new camp site for the first time, and also to have the medical responsibility for someone else's child.

To the English, King's Cross is an unromantic railway terminus in London. But to the SU movement in Scotland it is the idyllic site of a canvas camp on the Isle of Arran where, as Janice says, 'You look out of your tent in the morning and see the sea and the sun. It's brilliant!' But she has to admit that 'I've had my fair share of bad weather on Arran.'

Pointing people to Jesus

Janice prefers mixed camps to all-girl camps, and obviously finds it specially exhilarating to lead a camp which has attracted youngsters 'who've never been to church in their lives and who (having been asked to bring Bibles) come with Authorised Versions'.

She likes a mix of new campers and old hands. Sometimes they divide the campers into two groups for the evening sessions. One group is given basic Christian teaching; the other is for those who've heard a lot about the Christian faith already and want to move on. The young people choose which group they join.

'Young people don't rate themselves very highly'

To help leaders, SU Scotland's camps department in Glasgow sends out suggested series of talks, covering the topics 'Who is God?' 'Who is Jesus?' 'Who is the Holy Spirit?' 'What is sin?' 'How do we overcome the sin barrier?' and so on. 'I tend to be flexible and do my own thing,' says Janice. 'I feel strongly that I must keep pointing people to Jesus. I'm not sure they know so much about him and his love and patience and wisdom. By pointing people to Jesus we look at the whole issue of sin and forgiveness and the fact that Jesus is the Son of God.

'Young people don't rate themselves very highly. The Good News is that we can say to them "You're valuable", and that Jesus is willing to take them as they are. He doesn't expect them to change radically overnight. As they open themselves to him, he will change them.'

Janice has seen God powerfully at work.

She recalls a camp on Arran: 'A lot of young people were really touched by God.' She remembers a weekend event: 'I've never seen a team work so well together. God gave us tremendous unity. We were exploring areas of forgiving one another and caring for one another.'

One camp was attended by some young people who were quite hostile to the gospel and Janice tells of how their attitudes were changed. ' "Open the Bible? You must be joking!" But by the end of the week they were doing it.'

'So many children were making commitments'

Janice leads camps for primary as well as secondary school youngsters. During a 'praise time' at the end of a primary camp, the children were invited to share something that they had learned. One girl began to sing the song 'I'm special' and broke down in tears. 'I wrestled with what to do,' says Janice, 'but I chose to leave her. And as she sang that song, God touched her and made her realise that she really was special and that he had chosen her.

'At another primary camp, I was scared because so many children were making commitments to Christ.

'Manipulation is terrible. We have to be so careful to make sure that young people are not making commitments to please the leader or because this is what their friends are doing, but because they know Jesus has spoken to them. So I made it difficult for them. They had to come and see me at a quarter to eight in the morning. But the numbers who came – even on the last day – were staggering, and I know that some of these youngsters have gone on with God, and that this step was right for them.'

The security to ask questions

'SU's philosophy of camping is that a camp is a Christian community in which the team should reflect the love of Jesus. From a position of friendship we can share with young people who we are and what we believe. We can invite them to ask questions, and give them the security to ask questions that they wouldn't ask anywhere else. Yes, the philosophy works!

'No, I don't find it difficult to share the gospel.' But much is still expected of so-called 'full-time' Christian workers. 'An SU staff worker is expected to be that stage better as a Christian than the normal punter. And that's not true. We're all up against the same pressures. We all have sin to contend with. We're all weak. Some people reveal it – and some conceal it! The bottom line is that we're all weak and he is strong.'

You can't hide much from young people. 'They pick up whether you believe what you're teaching. So you have to be in tune with God.'

As an SU staff worker, Janice struggles the most with 'getting the balance right between being called and being driven.' She has a heavy work load. 'It's not easy to allow the right amount of time to prepare thoroughly, to pray and to read. The hardest thing is to know when to say "Yes" and when to say "No".

'I operate mainly from home. So it's difficult to switch off. I wrestle with this. And if you're new to an area, it's hard to establish a strong social life if you work antisocial hours.'

She doesn't rate driving a car the most enjoyable part of her job. 'I don't hate it but I don't love it.'

'That is so brilliant'

She enjoys working with colleagues and she's very grateful for their 'tremendous support', especially in her tough moments – which have included a car crash. And she appreciates not only the backing of so many praying friends but also SU's recommendation that every staff worker should put aside one day a month as a Quiet Day. And she does!

Reflecting on her life as a sharer of the Good News, she comments: 'It's a privilege that God is using you to change people. That is so brilliant.'

NO BASKING IN PAST GLORIES

Mona Chia

SINGAPORE

Mona Chia is a pastor's wife, the mother of two young children and Executive Director of Scripture Union Singapore. She is a Malaysian Chinese who was converted from agnosticism to Christianity whilst studying in England. 'I'd always believed in some kind of God, but I had no knowledge of who God was or is or how I could be in touch with him.'

A few weeks before she left Malaysia to study for her A-level exams in Birmingham, Mona had a visit from some Jehovah's Witnesses. 'They sparked my interest in the Christian God.'

When Mona arrived in England, a Christian girl called Hilary Clarke became her best friend. 'She and her family helped me to accept Christianity. They didn't speak to me evangelistically, but they spoke volumes by their actions.'

Mona found Christ – and also her racial identity

Hilary introduced Mona to the youth group of St John's, Harborne, and it was at that church at the end of an evangelistic sermon that Mona responded to an invitation to ask Jesus into her life.

At that stage, Mona admits, 'I didn't have a clear understanding of the cross and resurrection.' But that understanding grew. She moved on to another part of England to study for a science degree, and at the University of East Anglia, she linked up with the Christian Union, benefited from Bible teaching and pastoral care at a church in Norwich, and again experienced 'genuine love and hospitality' from Christian friends. Mona's commitment to Christ deepened. She realised that 'being fully committed wasn't just saying so but doing so'.

In England, Mona not only found Christ. She also found her racial identity. 'So often it is when we overseas-born Chinese go abroad that we really discover that we are not Western. At university I learned to be more Asian. I became President of the Oriental Society, to assert my own Chineseness and to help my peers of different backgrounds and heritage to accept Asians and Asian culture.

'I'm thankful that I became more conscious of my racial identity. But Christ has made us equal, and all our racial differences come to nothing when we are one in Christ.'

They exchanged secret notes in class

Mona first met her husband Kay Thiam – he also uses the name Chris – when they were six years old and together at kindergarten. Mona clearly remembers that when they were at the same primary school as eleven year olds, they used to exchange secret notes in class. She would write him a note saying 'I like you', and he would send a note back saying 'I like you too'.

But while Mona's parents paid for her to go to England to study, Chris went off to Australia, where he could get a free university education. When they were all those many miles from home and from each other, both of them found Christ – Mona in Birmingham, England, and Chris in Sydney, where he became a Christian during a Billy Graham Crusade.

They both graduated, and found that jobs were hard to come by in Malaysia, their home country. However, Mona was offered a job at the National University of Singapore, assisting with research on ultraviolet damage to eyes. Meanwhile, Chris had joined the staff of the Singapore newspaper, *Straits Times*, as a journalist.

'Deep down in my heart, I knew...'

So it was in Singapore that they met up again. For both of them, 'other relationships had been learning experiences'. But Mona confesses that, 'For a long time, I had secretly felt that Chris was the person for me. Deep down in my heart, I knew he was the best.'

They were married and went to Australia, Chris to study theology at Moore College in Sydney and Mona to work as a public relations consultant and then to study for her master's degree in business administration. They were both involved in work amongst Christian overseas students in Sydney and in evangelism on the campus of the University of New South Wales.

Mona was no stranger to Scripture Union. In Singapore, she had been a volunteer Bible club leader, committee member and team member at a children's camp. And it was while she and Chris were in Australia that Mona received a letter inviting her to be Executive Director of SU Singapore. Would she lead the SU staff team in their ministries to children, young people and families and in promoting Bible reading?

'Called from the ends of the earth'

Should she accept the invitation? As Mona recalls, 'Isaiah 41.9 and 10 convicted me!' The words, written in another context, that seemed so appropriate to her personally were these:

> I took you from the ends of the earth, from its farthest corners I called you.
> I said 'You are my servant.' I have chosen you and not rejected you.
> So do not fear, for I am with you; do not be dismayed, for I am your God.
> I will strengthen you and help you; I will uphold you with my righteous right hand.

So Mona became leader of SU Singapore's team of staff and volunteers as well as being a wife and a mother. Chris became a pastor at the Prinsep Street Presbyterian Church in Singapore. They have two young children, and a Filipino maid helps to look after them.

How does Mona keep a balance between her three roles? She reckons she is a wife first, a mother second, and an Executive Director third. But she confesses, 'I like sitting behind a desk thinking up strategies and I tend to forget to ring home. I'm conscious of that.'

'We have to break new ground'

Mona has written in Singapore's *SU News*, 'SU cannot bask in past glories, nor can we... wait for people to come knocking on our doors. We have to break new ground, to be out there telling people who we are and what we do.' Her vision for SU Singapore is to make SU known – through its publications and face-to-face ministries – in every Singaporean Christian home by the year 2000.

'Most importantly, we have to remember that it is God's love, not human love, that compels us and drives us to love our neighbours. Ultimately it is God who will make SU remain young, break new ground and grow.'

During her first year as Executive Director, she spoke at a number of children's meetings. She had not had any special training in children's ministry, but God gave her 'the tremendous encouragement of seeing fifty children accept Christ.' She readily acknowledges that she was 'the last person in a chain of events' leading to these commitments. 'But the Lord gave me this as a boost to my work at SU. 'Since then I've been concentrating on training other workers.'

From one brief visit to Singapore, I have begun to appreciate the context in which Mona and her colleagues are working. We saw a cricket match being played in the centre of the city, a reminder of its colonial past. But Singapore's economic achievements since independence have clearly been spectacular.

Those achievements are symbolised by its marvellous new Mass Rapid Transit (MRT) subway system, which we experienced, and which makes most of London's underground system look like something from the Dark Ages. The MRT is not only superbly efficient but also immaculately clean, so much so that you feel sorry for its cleaners, who, brooms in hand, are to be seen searching almost in vain for specks of dust.

Prosperity, but ...

You can cross a bridge now to all the recreational attractions of Sentosa island, where SU has had its own camp centre for many years, and where we saw mature palm trees being planted on a beach of golden sands by the side of a man-made lagoon. Singapore, in terms of income per head of population, is the second most prosperous country in Asia, after Japan.

'But with mounting affluence,' says Mona, 'there is amongst Singaporeans a growing pressure to succeed. Sometimes we seem to function on autopilot, not really questioning why we are working so hard.

'I am not saying that hard work and success are wrong, but ours is a materialistic and activity- and performance-oriented culture. We have lost touch with the relational aspects of life.'

'Children without childhood?'

'So children have computers and expensive watches, and they're ferried from tuition to a sports practice to a music lesson with only snippets of conversation in between.'

Mona put the question in Singapore's *SU News*: 'Is Singapore's child a child of mounting neurosis, pressure to achieve and rocketing spending habits?'

She quoted a report in the leading Singapore newspaper *Straits Times* that in the year 1992 government psychiatric clinics saw 1,211 child patients, twice the 1980s figure. And she points out that this figure of 1,211 doesn't include those who were seen at the many private clinics. She quoted another report which said that these children 'lack the spontaneity and playfulness that we associate with being a child. They're worried about the future like a stockbroker is worried about the next crash.'

That's why Mona and the Children and Families Ministries (CHIFAM) team initiated and organised an SU conference with the title 'Children without childhood?' (She confesses that the title was not original). She felt the need 'to alert Singapore parents and churches to what is happening to our children.

'We're thankful to the Lord that as a nation we're not experiencing war or deprivation, and that there may not be as much physical violence or sexual abuse in Singapore as elsewhere. But there's another kind of abuse when, by our own choice, we put unnecessary pressures on children so as to rob them of the joy of childhood.'

'Jesus used a child as a visual aid'

The conference attracted 200 participants. 'Childhood is not something that automatically accompanies children,' says its report. 'Childhood is about the character and quality of children's lives and life experience. Childhood is determined, planned and defined in terms of the life experiences adults provide for children. Childhood is dependent upon adults... whose nurture can be either caring, constructive and loving or, on the other hand, fear-instilling, destructive and hostile...

'Jesus used a child as a visual aid to challenge adults about entry into the kingdom of God... Each child is a person of worth...'

The two main conference speakers were SU leaders from Australia, well known for their expertise in children's ministry. 'Yes, there are cultural differences,' says Mona, 'but I believe the gospel transcends cultures. And if there are hard things to say, it's sometimes helpful if they're said by outsiders or consultants – particularly those who have seen the grief and pain from a post-materialistic viewpoint.'

The leaders of the eight workshops were all Singaporeans, who could relate what had been said in plenary sessions to the local cultural situation. Mona's husband Chris drew on his journalistic experience to lead a workshop on children and the media.

'We live in the information age,' he emphasised. 'And we get even more information because Singapore is one of the crossroads of the world. That's why we're so computer-oriented.' He asked whether children have the maturity to handle this bombardment of information. With cable television on its way in Singapore, he quoted a disturbing report from Germany. There a cable TV programme which was discovered to be soft porn had been watched by 50,000 viewers, many of them children under twelve.

Adults before their time?

Feedback from the conference was very encouraging, and a sequel was held. The speakers were all from within Singapore and the title was 'The hurried child'. Asks Mona, 'Are we trying to push children into being adults before their time? Children mustn't lose out on childhood as a time of wonderment, a time of trusting adults, a carefree time.'

Reflecting on these conferences, Mona points out that only a parachurch organisation like Scripture Union can provide an interdenominational arena like this. 'And we can ask people from the professional world who are Christians to share their expertise.'

'We must never squeeze God out'

'We have used these conferences to show biblical principles for a childhood into which God can enter. We must never squeeze God out, or allow computer games to squeeze out Bible reading. In this information age, the most vital information people need is the word of God and it is more urgent than ever that we promote the reading of the Bible.'

Traditionally, SU Singapore had majored on the nines to twelves, an age group that can respond more obviously to the gospel. But with the tendency to hurry children into adulthood, the movement is being called on more and more to work with younger age groups, including pre-schoolers.

'We don't do things the same way all the time'

Mona has certainly been breaking new ground. Why, I asked her, has she also organised children's carnivals? Why does SU Singapore get involved in arranging fun events of this kind?

'It's very important,' she says 'to raise our profile, particularly because in Singapore we're bombarded with so much information, so much competition for attention. We cannot continue an "in the closet" type work without telling people we exist. The carnival was a public relations exercise. Although it was very hard work, it was worth it. It provided an occasion for churches and Christian organisations to be united and to highlight further the needs of children and families today. The collective effort of seemingly different Christian groups was a powerful testimony indeed for the community.

'But events like this also provide a non-threatening environment where Christians can bring non-Christian families and have fun and make relationships as part of the evangelising process. And during the carnival, and throughout the day there are evangelistic programmes so that people can hear the gospel.'

SU Singapore has also organised charity events, such as a charity bike rally. 'Singapore is a fast-changing society, and people see that we don't do things the same way all the time. We are using our youthful energy to be aware of and concerned for the less privileged such as the elderly and the handicapped – the groups that our charter does not cover directly.

'Christians aren't fuddy-duddies. They don't just go to church all the time. They do other things that are meaningful and give pleasure.

Carnivals and charity treasure hunts are one-off events. And one-off events, says Mona, 'are good for publicity and good for preaching the gospel. But I'm conscious that they may not amount to anything unless there's also the long-term work of relationship building.

'I believe that our lives must be involved with people if they are really to come to know Jesus.'

BROWN WORLD, WHITE WORLD, BLACK WORLD

Daryl Henning, Mike Perks, Mgi Mabuza

SOUTH AFRICA

South Africa is a land of sunshine and superb scenery. It's also a land of barbed wire, barred windows and guard dogs. It has more luxury houses than I've ever seen before in my life. It also has many thousands of shacks, usually made of scrap materials and often of rusty corrugated iron. The shacks are quite often on our TV screens; the luxury houses hardly ever.

It's hard to realise that rich and poor in South Africa are living on the same planet.

I'd never realised until I visited there how successful the apartheid system was in creating entirely separate worlds in South Africa – a white world (with black servants and waiters), a brown world and a black world.

Daryl on the edges of two worlds

Daryl Henning has lived on the edges of two of those separate worlds. Daryl is a so-called Cape coloured (i.e. of mixed race) and is SU's Associate Regional Director in the Western Cape. His personal story speaks eloquently of the hurts and the hopes of South Africa.

I first met Daryl some five or six years ago on a chill, damp late November evening at Liverpool Street Station in London, which must then (before its totally transforming refurbishment) have been the grimiest and grottiest railway terminus in Britain. Daryl and his friend Jeremy

Ganga had flown from South Africa to Luxemburg, made their way to the Hook of Holland, crossed the North Sea to Harwich and then come into London by train. Not the most glamorous of approach routes...

We remembered that bleak November night when we sat together in Daryl's office in the sunshine of Cape Town and I listened to the story of his life.

'My dad is white and my mother is coloured. So in the days of apartheid, though they had a church ceremony, they were married illegally.'

They lived on what was a border line under the Group Areas Act between a 'white' area and a 'coloured' area. There were whites living on one side of the road and coloureds on the other.

'Family ashamed because of my skin colour'

The problem of mixed marriages, as Daryl pointed out, is 'that you never know what the kids are going to look like'. It turned out that Daryl's brother and sister had fairer skins, and were accepted as white, whereas he was darker.

'My family were ashamed of me because of the colour of my skin. Sometimes, when people called at the house, they even locked me up in the kitchen. My brother called me all kinds of names. I went to a coloured school and I was never allowed to bring my school friends home.

'My mother was torn between her love for my dad and her love for me.'

When Daryl was about to leave school, and had applied to study law, his family hit financial problems. That meant that there was no money to pay for his studies, and he had to get a job straight away.

Then his dad moved into a white area. 'So I was living there illegally. I ran away from home.'

Earlier, when he was thirteen or fourteen, Daryl had made a simple commitment to Christ after watching a Christian movie. But now, as an eighteen year old, he went to church and was again challenged with the gospel – and to a deeper commitment.

'I love you and I forgive you'

He vividly recalls that experience. 'The light was switched on because I understood God's love as I'd never understood it before. I understood God's acceptance of who I was. Jesus had died for me – and that made sense.

'So then I had to go back home and start talking to my dad and mum. My dad was the first person I spoke to. I said, "I want you to know that I love you and that I forgive you." And that was the start of a healing process.'

'I was completely swept off my feet'

How did Daryl meet up with Wendy, who is now his wife?

'I met her at an over–20s club at church. The club was really a social excuse for people who couldn't find a boyfriend or a girlfriend.

'My job was to keep the place clean, and I was there with my broom on the night Wendy came in.'

But the sweeping that night was of a different kind. 'I was completely swept off my feet. I instantly planned to meet her and found out her phone number. She was doing a Bible study on Romans. She asked me to give her some notes to help her. I've never given her those notes. She's still waiting for them.

'The competition for Wendy was fast and furious. I was a Bible college student with not a cent in my pocket. I had no transport. But we competed and she very wisely chose me!

'My main rival was also a Christian.' But Daryl had a very useful ally. 'Wendy's mother let me know that she preferred me.'

One day there was what Daryl describes as 'a big showdown'. He and his main rival turned up at Wendy's house together, and they sat in the room looking at each other. After a while, Daryl confesses, 'I outstared him and he left.

'Wendy and I dated one another for four years before we married.'

Wendy works as a primary school teacher. Daryl himself, as SU's Associate Regional Director, heads up the field work in the Western Cape, which for SU's ministries is divided into seven areas. In each area there's an SU worker, and each worker has the help of a Trendsetter, a short-term volunteer.

'The first non-white person to speak in a school'

'I love working with kids. I also see myself as a bridge-builder. I've often been the first non-white person to speak in a school. So the talk I give is more than just a talk.' Daryl emphasises that he is not only communicating the Good News of the gospel in words. By his very presence on the platform in the school hall, he's demonstrating that part of the Good News is that all races are of equal worth in the sight of God.

For many years Scripture Union has held multi-racial camps in South Africa, and it's at these camps that attitudes have been seen to change most rapidly and most radically.

'Often I've been the first non-white person to lead an activity. Non-whites think, "One of our guys is leading this. This is fantastic!" A white kid once said to me, "Are you a coloured guy?" And when I told him I was, he said, "I would never have known it!"

'At one of our camps, two blacks, two coloureds and two whites (one of them Afrikaans-speaking) were to sleep in the same dormitory. And they'd never been in the same room as people of other races before. The first night, they looked at each other gingerly. One guy asked if he could be moved into another room, but we wouldn't allow this.

'I watched this group. By the fourth or fifth day of the camp, they were all jumping into the swimming pool together, not thinking about the colour of their skins.'

Daryl finds that young South Africans of all races are very open to the gospel. 'We have tremendous opportunities. There's a searching.' And amidst all the political changes, 'We're in the business of offering eternal answers.'

Not all the uncertainties that face young South Africans are political. 'I've worked in a white school,' says Daryl, 'where eighty per cent of the kids come from broken homes.'

'God loves us and accepts us regardless...'

The coloured community has to cope with the problems of low self-esteem and the lack of a clear identity. Daryl admits, 'I'm still struggling with these issues myself. I'm still battling with the questions "Who am I?" and "Where do I belong?"'

So what is the Good News, I asked him, for the coloured community? 'That's a tough question,' was his reply. Daryl knows the great truths that God loves us and accepts us regardless of the colour of our skin and that those who trust in Jesus belong to the biggest and best family in the world. And he not only knows these great truths; he also fearlessly proclaims them. But he is honest enough to admit that despite all that, his struggles and doubts are not over.

It's hardly surprising that Daryl has his personal struggles. But he also has many encouragements, especially in the friendship evangelism which is at the heart of SU's camping ministry. He told me one story that could have happened almost anywhere in the world.

'During one of our camps, there was one young man who was very quietly watching me. After a few days, he blurted out, "You've got to be a Scorpio!" He thought that was what made me different!'

'I'm ready now!'

'I explained that this wasn't the reason for the difference! We got talking about the gospel, and on the last evening of the camp, I encouraged him to accept Christ as his Saviour and Lord. But he told me that he wasn't ready to do this!'

Daryl admits that in his earlier days he might have written off that conversation as a failure. But he would have been wrong!

'A week later, the young man phoned me and said "I'm ready now!" So I led him to the Lord over the phone.

And that guy has gone on to be one of our camp leaders.'

'Attitudes will only change through friendship'

To be hopeful about individual people you know is one thing. To be hopeful about the future of your country is another. Is Daryl hopeful about the future of South Africa?

'You've got to be hopeful!' He is very aware from his own experience that South Africa needs more than a new constitution and a new flag. There must also be a change in attitudes – and that is going to be 'a long, slow, painful process'. Against the background of his experience of SU's multi-racial camps, he believes strongly that 'attitudes will only change through friendship.'

Speaking as a Christian who is actively involved in working to bring about this change in attitudes, he adds from deep conviction, 'I'm hopeful because of the message we carry, and because God is with us.'

Daryl has lived on the edge of South Africa's brown and white worlds. Tragically few white South Africans have ever entered the world of the black townships. When my wife told our white coach driver on our tourist trip from Cape Town to Port Elizabeth that we had visited Langa and other black townships in the Western Cape, he was amazed. He asked if we'd had police permission. And having carefully stated that the opinions he expressed in this conversation were his own and not that of his coach company, he said, 'All the people in Langa are criminals or Communists!'

Taking coachloads of white students into black townships

Mike Perks, our white SU colleague who is SU's Regional Director in Port Elizabeth, reckons that ninety-seven per cent of white South Africans have never been into a black township in their lives, unless they've gone in as policemen or soldiers.

Mike makes a practice of taking a coachload of white student leaders of school Christian groups into one of the black townships around Port Elizabeth. He does this as part of their training. His line is 'You're growing up in South Africa. If you're going to be an effective leader, you need to know and understand a little of the background of the people in the townships.' The white students are given the unique opportunity of getting out of their coach, and standing in the main square with all its market stalls – and visiting some of the homes.

'For most of them, it's their first ever experience of going into a township. And when we tell them that this is where we're going, you can see the nervousness written all over their faces. Afterwards, they tell us how scared they were.

'They wonder if people are going to jeer at them or even throw stones at them. And they're always absolutely amazed at the friendly welcome that we get. The people in the township just start clapping and singing and dancing. It's a real encouragement to them, too, to see white young people make the effort to visit them for a change.'

'We're only just recovering from the Anglo-Boer War'

But prejudice in South Africa is not only white against black and black against white. In relationships between Afrikaaners and English-speaking whites, Mike points out that in some areas 'We're only just recovering from the Anglo-Boer War of a century ago. In that war, the British put Boer women and children into concentration camps, burned their farms and took away their freedom. And you can be sure that those Boers will have told their children about that – and their grandchildren. It's only now, when we've got as far as their great-grandchildren, that the memory is being erased.'

Time is often said to be a great healer. It's also been proved – in South Africa as elsewhere – to be a very slow one, taking generations. And the breaking down of prejudice between blacks and whites could take generations more. But the gospel and the influence of gospel people as salt and light can do wonders to speed up the process. And Mike, who has travelled around quite a bit, believes God has called him to be in South Africa at this time.

How did Mike come to commit his own life to Christ? 'Until recently, I'd have said that this was at a Scripture Union camp when I was thirteen. At that camp I had an incredible knowledge that God was talking to me and asking me to give my life to him. My life was turned upside down. With my exuberant personality, I became a very radical young Christian.

'But looking back now, I can recall the time one year earlier when our Sunday school teacher asked us to stay behind at the end of the meeting if we wanted to follow Jesus. Three of us did so, and very nervously our teacher led us to the Lord.

'Looking back still further, I can remember sitting on my bed with my mother and saying that I wanted Jesus to be my friend. My own experience of working with children has reminded me that I started making responses to Jesus when I was seven or eight.

'This has had a real impact on my understanding of children's evangelism. So often people accept a child's physical, mental and emotional growth, but forget that they also develop spiritually. I don't believe there is a time when a child suddenly becomes spiritually accountable. We have to help the child to grow in a natural pattern of development, making responses to God at his or her own level of understanding. We mustn't demand too much or expect too little.

'How do we know what is an appropriate response? By the guidance of the Holy Spirit and through the level of relationship that we have built up with the child.'

Before he became a youth evangelist, Mike qualified as a chartered accountant. A turning point in his life came when he attended a conference of Methodist leaders.

An accountant in tears

For some while, Mike's friends had been dropping hints such as 'When are you going to start preaching?' And on the last day of this conference, 'The minister upfront asked people to go forward if they felt God was calling them to "full-time" service.

'I remember deciding to stand still. I wasn't going forward. That was my firm resolve.

'But I suddenly found myself upfront, crying in my minister's arms. I don't remember going forward. It was as if the Lord had moved me there. And the release of tension was marvellous.'

An accountant crying...? Well, this one did.

Mike believes that his style of evangelistic ministry stems from his own experience as a teenager. 'For me sharing the gospel comes out of a real sense of growing up at school with an inferiority complex.' Despite his exuberance, especially amongst Christian friends, 'I wasn't sure of myself at all when relating to my "secular" peers. I didn't play rugby and if you didn't play rugby, you were nothing. I was also very uncomfortable in relating to girls, especially because of one or two bad experiences of rejection!'

'Released to be the person Christ wants you to be'

'That's why in sharing the gospel, I speak about people being special. I say, "You can be released to be the person Christ wants you to be. You don't have to conform to anybody else's expectations."

'I've become very aware of meeting people as individuals rather than en masse. I remember how an SU camp leader led me to Christ. In all my training sessions, I urge leaders when they invite a young person to commit his life to Christ to say "Is this something you would like to do now, or would you like to think about it?" Let the individual decide, without pressure, as the Holy Spirit works in his life.

'Evangelism that is pressurised is not lasting evangelism. Whether young people are black or white or coloured, you must find out where they are hurting and meet them at that point of need.'

Mike himself confesses to having had hurts in his own life, especially in a series of girlfriends, with whom he seemed to make no progress at all. 'I'd become exasperated, and tense about not being able to find someone to marry. But I went to a camp where Michael Cassidy of African Enterprise spoke about giving up your "Isaacs", giving up what you treasure most. And the Lord spoke into my life and I decided that if the Lord wanted me to remain single, I would do that. The Lord would have to show me very clearly that this was his will, and equip me and change my hormones substantially!'

'You must meet Barbie'

That didn't prove necessary. 'I took Barbie out on a long-standing date that Saturday. Six weeks later we were engaged, and six months later we were married at the Scripture Union camp site at Stoney Ridge near Johannesburg. We had a "camp wedding" with many of the guests staying overnight.'

Mike and Barbie had met one another at the Scripture Union office in Johannesburg. She was a secretary there. 'As a voluntary worker, I was organising SU camps, particularly hiking camps, and the folk in the office said "You must meet Barbie. She enjoys hikes, too."

'Barbie used to help in the bookshop. So I bought a tremendous amount of books.

'We'd be in a room with the other staff, and five minutes later we'd find ourselves alone. The rest of the office were trying to get Barbie married off to me. And it worked! We have a superb relationship and a superb marriage. We have had some pretty tough times, but our love grows deeper by the year, despite the pressures of ministry.'

Lots of black playmates – but Mike was the boss

Even though Mike had grown up in a home that was relatively liberal, both politically and in racial attitudes, he still found himself growing up with a typically superior white attitude. 'A hundred people lived on our farm. I had lots and lots of black playmates. But I was the boss. If I said "We'll play cricket", we played cricket. If I said they should go home, they went home. The whole relationship was one of master and servant.

'This superiority/inferiority thing is in our upbringing. Many blacks think they are inferior because they have been brought up to believe that. If you're white, you've been brought up hearing racist jokes about blacks and why you can't trust black people. All your life you've heard "Give a black anything, and he'll break it" ... And if you're black, you've always seen that the top jobs, the status and the lovely homes belong to the whites.

'To overcome these prejudices is a tough challenge.

'Most whites, including myself, condemned blacks for burning down a school, for example. I don't condone that, but as I developed deeper relationships and heard about their experiences in black education, I began to understand their frustrations and why it happened.

'Nathi Vika, my first black SU colleague here in the Eastern Cape, helped me to think through these issues. And my friendship with Sandile Mntoninshi, his successor, is such that we can talk freely and openly.'

A learning experience when Nathi disappeared

'It was a learning experience for me when Nathi disappeared for three weeks. He went to a family funeral in the Transkei. They tend to be fairly lengthy affairs. When he finally got back, I found out for the first time that he had two sons in self-imposed exile. This was in the days when the African National Congress was still banned, and Nathi had been up to Zambia and Tanzania to see his sons. He helped me to understand that he'd been away through circumstances that were beyond his control.

'It also helped me as a white South African to see that exiles were real people, with families that missed them. The apartheid years brought much grief to many families. But as a white, this experience had been distant from me, until I started to develop relationships with blacks.

'I believe that the fact that SU continued to employ

Nathi, at a time when the ANC weren't even allowed to be quoted at all in the newspapers, helped people to realise that SU was serious in its move towards being a truly non-racial movement.

'This is a constant challenge to SU and in our evangelism in the townships.

'I think I've also been able to help black people to understand white fears and prejudices.'

Multi-racial camps

How is the programme at SU's multi-racial evangelistic camps for young people – for example, at 'Breakaway at Woodridge' – influenced by the racial mix and by the political situation in South Africa?

'The basic gospel message always remains the same: God's love, our sin, that Jesus died and came back to life and that he is the way to salvation and forgiveness, and our need to respond to God.'

But the programme has to take account of cultural differences. Because SU in South Africa began in the white community, 'much of our camping ethos comes from that community. For example, a lot of our humour tends to be white humour. Another example is that black kids are used to church services that go on for hours and hours, whereas in our Western culture we work to a strict time schedule – and if you go over time, people start looking at their watches. They say whites have watches, blacks have time!

'Last year, we had an African evening. We all sat on the floor and ate a traditional Xhosa meal. For many whites this was a valuable learning experience they would not have had anywhere else.'

Workshops on prayer – and on South Africa's constitution

'At Woodridge we aim at a balanced programme. We have workshops on the Holy Spirit and on prayer, on being a teenager and on sexual relationships – and on South Africa, on the issues of prejudice, understanding violence, and writing a new constitution for our country. In addition, we have plenty of fun and try and stretch the kids physically.

'One of the struggles for white kids is that because they live in a privileged society, they don't feel the injustices of South Africa. Generally, very little has affected their lifestyle, as unrest and turmoil have effectively been limited to the township areas.'

Telling blacks they're equal – and whites they're not superior

Do you have to emphasise to them that God made all human beings equal? 'Yes, we have to tell the black children that they're special and that they're equal. And the whites that they're not superior, but just the same as everybody else.

'We've got to help blacks to see that out of their hurt and pain and disadvantage there is hope in Jesus Christ. Man-made political solutions won't solve everything. We also have to change hearts. But it is not only black children that we have to meet at their point of need.

'At one of our Breakaway at Woodridge camps, there was a girl who'd been sponsored by the welfare authorities. She had a very sad background. She wasn't an easy person to cope with at camp, and at one point she reduced her exasperated group leader to tears.

'On the last night, we have a session called "Kids say so", when we give the young people the opportunity to say what Jesus has done in their lives. There's always a queue of campers waiting to speak. And during this meeting, this girl stood up in front of about 180 people and said that she'd never had people who'd loved and cared for her. She went on: "I've never in my life ever had anybody I could trust. People have always let me down. But now I have a friend in Jesus whom I really can trust and who will never let me down."

'That for me is how evangelism should work – out of a relationship where a leader has lived out her Christianity.'

During the apartheid years, four separate organisations

ran school Christian groups in black schools, coloured schools, white English-speaking schools and white Afrikaans-speaking schools. But now these organisations are exploring ways of coming together and Scripture Union is running training courses for school Christian group leaders across the racial barriers – and is being invited to run school groups in every sector of the community, especially where no groups are yet operating.

Soweto wasn't even marked on our map

By mid-1993 there were SU groups in sixty primary and secondary schools in Soweto, where we were given a marvellous and memorable welcome at the Scripture Union office by Mgi Mabuza and his colleagues.

Soweto, the biggest and best-known of all South Africa's black townships, has a population of around two million. So naturally, when we bought a map of South Africa in our tourist travels, we looked it up to check where it was. To our amazement (though not to the surprise of our black friends), Soweto wasn't even shown on the map, though many smaller 'white' places were marked in bold type. Obviously, South Africa's cartographers have lived in the white world.

Stabbed by one of a rival teenage gang

When Mgi Mabuza was a teenager in Soweto, he belonged to a gang. It wasn't political. It was just a teenage gang.

But one evening, he was stabbed by a member of a rival gang and taken to hospital unconscious. At school earlier that day, 'A Christian lady had taught us a song with a chorus "I have decided to follow the Lord". It sank deep down in my heart. And when I woke up in hospital, this chorus kept ringing in my mind. I knew I had not decided to follow. But the chorus was singing deep down within me.'

Two weeks later, 'while the stab wound was still fresh', Mgi was invited to a Teen Challenge camp. 'It was free. I thought it would be an adventure to go there. I didn't know it was an appointment with the Lord.' And it was at that camp – the first Christian camp he had attended – that Helmut Mgi Mabuza came to Christ.

But he resisted the message of the gospel and the challenges of the camp speakers until the last service on the very last day of the camp. And the reason he resisted was a girl called Eve.

'We met at high school during our student days in June 1973. We were truly head over heels in love. In our school's student circles we were amongst the top three best known going steady couples. When I went off to the Teen Challenge camp, we'd been involved together for exactly a year. Our love was at its peak.

'Accepting Christ would mean a break with the one I loved'

'So what really made me resist so vigorously the challenge to commit my life to Christ? It was my hot commitment to the only lady I've ever loved! She was also dearly committed to me. And I realised that my acceptance of Christ would mean one thing: a definite break with Eve. I dreaded the thought! How would life be without her? Besides, how would I ever approach her with the story? I couldn't imagine the damage it would do to the poor girl.

'But then the last service came and swept me off my two feet. What a tremendous experience! What an unspeakable joy I felt! Then I told myself that Eve had never felt the joy or encountered the experience I was going through...

'But what then? The practical reality of breaking with Eve was glaring me straight in the eye. I had to do it. And I did it.

'My Christian mentor, the one who had invited me to the camp, found me crying at home as I tore up and burnt Eve's love letters. The Lord made me bold enough to approach Eve with my story the following day.

'She told me later (and her mother confirmed this) that after she had heard my news, she lay flat on her bed and was ill for the rest of the week. Life became meaningless to her.'

But three months later...

'To cut a long story short, three months later she committed her life to Christ at a student conference. A year after that, I asked her to marry me.'

Mgi and his wife Eveness Matshidiso (those are her full names) have three children – a son, Sibusiso (which means 'a blessing'), and two daughters, Africa Hlengiwe (which means 'redeemed') and Vera-Mae, Duduzile (which means 'comforter').

Mgi's parents were churchgoers, and they lived with his brothers and sisters in Soweto. But Mgi spent much of his early life in the township of Tembisa, east of Johannesburg and not far from Alexandra. He explains why.

'My uncle and aunt did not have a son. So, in accordance with our culture, they took me to grow up with them.' They followed the traditional religion, and Helmut Mgi went through an initiation ceremony, going to the *nyanga*, who claims to be in touch with spiritual forces. The ceremony involves making cuts with a razor blade, either on the wrists or at the bottom of the neck, and inserting a kind of medicine.'

Matchbox houses – and hostels for migrant workers

Most of the two million or so Sowetans live in the so-called matchbox houses that we have seen on television. But Soweto is not quite as uniform as its TV image suggests. Some of its people exist grimly in squalid shacks. Others have improved their matchboxes by diligent DIY. And a very, very few live in luxury homes.

Yet domestic rubbish lines many of Soweto's streets. To the visitor, this vast township, which seems to go drably on and on, is a stark contrast to nearby Johannesburg's leafy 'white' suburbs. Perhaps grimmest of all are Soweto's hostels for migrant workers – row upon row of them. These are places where men are obliged to live hundreds of miles apart from their families: they are also centres of political anger and unrest.

I was invited to look briefly inside one section of one of the hostels. It housed sixteen men, four to a cubicle. Each occupant had a mattress on a brick base and a small locker containing a paraffin cooker. There was a kitchen area where the initials 'IFP' (Inkhata Freedom Party) were scratched on the wall, with tables and a boiler to keep the place warm in the winter – and that was about all. Running water and washing and toilet facilities were across the yard.

'Even so-called Communists struggle not to believe...'

In this vast township of Soweto, which has so often been centre stage in South African politics, Scripture Union runs school SU groups 'with no hindrance', Mgi emphasises, 'from the authorities or the students or the radicals.'

The usual pattern is that on the day when the voluntary SU group meets, the staff member goes into the school to speak to all the students and teachers at the morning assembly. Then in the afternoon he runs games and activities with the SU group and applies the teaching at morning assembly more personally.

Christianity is the generally accepted religion in Soweto, and the majority of the population are church attenders. 'We don't have the problem of atheism,' says Mgi. 'The fact of the existence of God is a foregone conclusion in the black community. Even the so-called Communists amongst us struggle not to believe in God.'

'The God of justice for all sent his Son to die for all'

'The problem we do have is that of the "white God". It is the problem of the "clean God" who does not want to "dirty" himself with issues affecting the community.

'Our mission is to cleanse people's ideas of God from all he has been tainted with, by both blacks and whites to suit their likings, all along the years. We've got to present him as he is – the God of justice for all: black, white and brown. As the God who sent his Son to come and die for all. And we are proud of Scripture Union's contribution to bridging the gap between the races.'

And at morning school assemblies in Soweto, SU workers are able not only to present the God of justice, the God who sent his Son to die for all, as he really is. They are also able to appeal for a response. 'Parents and school authorities are happy with that, because they would like to see changes in the students. Although they themselves won't respond readily, they would like the students to respond!

Sharing your lunch in Christ's name

'Teachers feel they need someone who can come in and have a positive influence on the students.' But Mgi makes the point very firmly that 'We don't see the gospel as just for children and students!' And he tells the story of a student who was addressing a school assembly and said courageously, 'I'm not speaking to students only but to everyone who has ears to hear!'

When SU staff take a primary school assembly in Soweto, there's usually a ten-minute time limit. So what are they able to do? To give an example, 'We tell the story of the boy who had the lunch-box that was used by Jesus. Now in our situation, there are those who have something and those who have nothing. So we say, "If you have your lunch-box, and are willing to share with others around you in the name of the Lord..."'

Mgi sees the voluntary school SU group as a means of evangelism. 'It's an open group. But of course it also becomes a "home" for the Christians in the school.'

Camping 'out of the urban noise of Soweto'

SU Soweto also has a vigorous camping programme. But, although they have the right weather for it, they never camp under canvas. Mgi explains why. 'Tents have been identified with soldiers. And soldiers have been regarded as the enemies of the people.'

They take the children 'out of the urban noise of Soweto' to a beautiful site in the mountains 'so that they can begin to appreciate God's creation.'

In a typical camp day, there's the usual mixture of games, workshops and Christian teaching and worship. Mgi says emphatically, 'We believe that children should have fun in our camps.' It's also very much part of Mgi's (and SU's) camping philosophy that 'To win the right to speak to anyone, you must be acquainted with his politics. And children's politics are their games.'

'You must be willing to crawl on your knees'

He believes that every SU camp leader needs to be trained – and trained not only to do such things as leading a Bible reading group, but also in how to relate to children.

'We need to be able to get down to their level.' Mgi means that literally! 'You must be willing to crawl on your knees. Then they will see a friend in you and will share their problems because you have already won their confidence.'

He also believes that every camp leader needs to be trained 'to be open-minded'. What does he mean by that? He gives an example. 'There's a problem amongst conservative Christians that they will talk about not getting involved in politics. If you say that to young people who are highly political, you close their minds to the Christian faith altogether.

'You must be sensitive and listen to young people and take in what they say and put your gospel around what they are saying. There are very good things in what they say. Capitalise on the good and leave out what is wrong.'

'Whites pray in turn. We find that rather slow and boring.'

SU South Africa began as a ministry to English-speaking whites. But its image is changing, and the movement is being increasingly accepted by the black population. 'We're doing things our way,' says Mgi. 'For example, when whites pray together, individuals pray in turn while the others listen. We find that rather slow and boring. So we all pray simultaneously.'

So how far do Sowetans see Scripture Union as their movement?

'SU has established its credibility here,' says Mgi. 'Otherwise we wouldn't have survived, especially in times of turmoil like these. We have never been labelled as targets, as have some companies that are run by white people. We are accepted not only by the community but also by the so-called political organisations.'

How have they achieved this acceptance? 'We invite our neighbours in and explain what we are doing in schools. And we get involved in what is happening in the community. We open our offices for street meetings to discuss community problems.

'We are Sowetans,' says Mgi proudly. 'When the teachers march, we are there, too. And when I go into a school, they say "Mgi, we saw you on the march." '

Presenting God as he really is

'Our struggle as blacks has been a struggle for justice. Justice is all about reconciliation. What we in the black community are praying for is that our white counterparts will be open to the hand of friendship that we are offering to them. We blacks make up the majority in this country. And if the majority is saying "We must live together as human beings. . . ." '

So, as the future of South Africa unfolds, Mgi and Mike and Daryl and their colleagues are praying and working for reconciliation as they seek to present God as he really is – in Mgi's words, 'the God of justice for all, black, white and brown, the God who sent his Son to come and die for all.'